PEOPLE *of the* STURGEON

PEOPLE *of the* STURGEON

Wisconsin's Love Affair with an Ancient Fish

KATHLEEN SCHMITT KLINE   RONALD M. BRUCH   FREDERICK P. BINKOWSKI

WITH PHOTOGRAPHS BY BOB RASHID

WISCONSIN HISTORICAL SOCIETY PRESS

Published by the Wisconsin Historical Society Press
Publishers since 1855

© 2009 The Board of Regents of the University of Wisconsin System

Paperback edition 2018

This book was funded in part by the University of Wisconsin Sea Grant Institute under grants from the National Sea Grant College Program, National Oceanic & Atmospheric Administration, U.S. Department of Commerce, and from the State of Wisconsin (Federal grant #NA060AR4170011, #NA16RG2257, and #NA14OAR4170092 Project No.C/C-1.)

This book was also funded in part by the Wisconsin Sturgeon Spearing License Fund and by a grant from Sturgeon For Tomorrow.

wisconsin**history**.org

22 21 20 19 18   5 4 3 2

The Library of Congress has cataloged the hardcover edition as follows:

Kline, Kathleen Schmitt.
  People of the sturgeon : Wisconsin's love affair with an ancient fish / Kathleen Schmitt Kline, Ronald M. Bruch, Frederick P. Binkowski ; with photographs by Bob Rashid.
    p. cm.
  Includes bibliographical references and index.
  ISBN 978-0-87020 -431-9 (hardcover : alk. paper) 1. Lake sturgeon—Wisconsin. 2. Lake sturgeon fisheries—Wisconsin. 3. Lake sturgeon—Conservation—Wisconsin. I. Bruch, Ronald M. II. Binkowski, Frederick P. III. Title.
  QL638.A25K55 2009
  597.4209775—dc22
                               2009004104

in memory of **Bob Rashid**, *1949–2008*

Acknowledgments

We are grateful to everyone whose assistance, expertise, and support was invaluable to the success of this project, including: Richard and Patricia Braasch; Bill and Kathy Casper; Darlene Czeskleba; Dan Folz; Dan and Gloria Groeschel; Wayne Hoelzel; Andy Horn; Dick Koerner; Vic and Mary Lou Schneider; Lisa Sharkey, Mike Staggs, George Boronow, Ron Kazmierczak, and Todd Schaller of the Wisconsin Department of Natural Resources; Ruth Olson of the University of Wisconsin–Madison Center for the Study of Upper Midwestern Cultures; Scott Cross, Brad Larson, and Joan Lloyd of the Oshkosh Public Museum; Anders Andren, Jim Hurley, Mary Lou Reeb, Elizabeth White, Stephen Wittman, and Tina Yao of the University of Wisconsin Sea Grant Institute; Val Klump of the University of Wisconsin–Milwaukee Great Lakes WATER Institute; Kathy Borkowski, Diane Drexler, John Motoviloff, and Kate Thompson of the Wisconsin Historical Society Press; and Rebecca Alegria, David Grignon, and Don Reiter of the Menominee Indian Tribe of Wisconsin. Our special thanks to Bob Rashid for his rich photographs that really made this book come to life. We are especially grateful to Holly Cohn for her assistance with the project after Bob's sudden death. We all miss him.

We also thank two groups that have contributed so much to the health of the Winnebago sturgeon population and the public commitment to preserving it. Hundreds of state employees have worked tirelessly to protect the Winnebago sturgeon since the management program began in 1903, and the commitment continues today through long days and nights spent by biologists and wardens during spearing and spawning seasons. In addition, for over thirty years, Sturgeon For Tomorrow has raised and donated over $700,000 for sturgeon research and management, and its three thousand members have helped to elevate public awareness about effective lake sturgeon management. Our hats are off to all of these dedicated sturgeon enthusiasts for their important contributions toward making the Winnebago sturgeon population the success story it is today.

STURGEON TAGGING CREW 1

(Front row): Jack O'Brien, Dan Folz, Debbie Folz, Lee Meyers; (Standing, back row): Elliot Hoffman, Mike Jungwirth, Cory Wienandt, Mike Penning, Paul Cain (Hainy), Ron Bruch, Bob Marin (Hermie), Rob Lauer, Tom Thuemler

STURGEON TAGGING CREW 2

(Kneeling): Kendall Kamke, Dave Bartz; (Standing): Chad Shirey, Nick Starzi, Doug Rinzel, Tom Sinclair, Carlos Echevarria, Dave Paynter, Jaclyn Zelko, John Paynter, Paul Bednarek, Edwin Scott

STURGEON FOR TOMMOROW
Main Chapter Directors

Sitting: Bill Casper, Lloyd Lemke, Dan Groeschel; Standing: Andy Horn, Tim Simon

STURGEON FOR TOMMOROW
Upper Lakes Chapter Directors

Sitting: Sally Gilson, John Buttke, Dave Lamers Standing: Brian Loker, Mike Will, Dana Woods, Matt Woods

STURGEON FOR TOMMOROW
Northern Half Chapter Directors

Sitting: Eugene Herubin, Wayne Hoelzel; Standing: Steve Karow

STURGEON FOR TOMMOROW
Southwestern Chapter Directors

Sitting: Glenn Ninneman, Gary Ninneman, Linda Wendt, Lee Patt, Jim Patt; Standing: Shawn Wendt, Craig Freiberg, Paul Muche

STURGEON FOR TOMMOROW
West Central Chapter Directors

Sitting: Mary McAloon, Sylvia Epprecht, Jill Epprecht, Sandy Ristow, Keith Berholtz; Standing: Richard Braasch, Patricia Braasch, Bob Marin, Ryan Epprecht, Dick Ristow, Ron Epprecht

Contents

PEOPLE *of the* STURGEON

ANCIENT SURVIVORS 1

Ron Bruch checks in with other DNR employees stationed around Lake Winnebago to find out how many sturgeon have been speared that day. Bruch has led the management of the Winnebago sturgeon population since 1990.

Previous page: Sturgeon are ancient survivors. According to fossil records, they have been on Earth for at least one hundred fifty million years. This map shows the present-day range of the world's twenty-seven species of sturgeon.

It's 9:30 a.m. on Saturday—a chilly, dull, February day in Wisconsin. It's the kind of day when you could pop your head out of an ice shack and not be sure if it's morning or late afternoon. Ron Bruch is circling Lake Winnebago in his pickup truck, making the rounds to all of the registration stations dotted around the lake, many of them in the parking lots of local bars and restaurants. He pulls into Wendt's on the Lake, where he raps on the door of a tiny, heated trailer and heads inside to chat with the state Department of Natural Resources (DNR) workers. The small space is teeming with jokes, fish stories, and five-alarm chili. Ron helps himself to all of it. It's the second weekend of spearing season, and everyone seems to be in high spirits, especially Ron.

Back in the truck, he tunes the radio to 1530 AM, where Jerry Schneider is rolling out polka music all morning long and broadcasting news of successful spearings in between tunes. "When I was a boy, we'd spend our summers up north in Butternut, where my family is from," Ron says as he turns down the joyful cries of a concertina. "My dad and I would go fishing for walleye on the Flambeau River, and every now and then we'd see a sturgeon jump out of the water. It really made an impression on me. But never in my wildest dreams did I ever think I'd be working with them like this."

In fact, Ron's position is one of only a handful of such jobs in the entire world—managing a self-sustaining population of sturgeon, healthy enough for an annual season of recreational fishing or, in Wisconsin's case, spearing. Across the globe, in Russia and Iran, sturgeon are pursued for their eggs, the source of an exotic delicacy to be enjoyed by the wealthy. But here in Wisconsin, lake sturgeon belong to everyone, and they're revered for what they are and have been for millions of years: a tough, old fish.

"A few years ago I was at one of the registration stations, and one of the guys who came in—Don Burg from Stockbridge—told us about how his great-uncle used to spear with the Stockbridge Indians on Lake Winnebago in the early 1900s," Ron continues. "I went home that night thinking about what a great story that was and how there are probably a lot more memories and stories out there that might be lost if we don't collect them."

At another stop along the lake, a man in Carhartt overalls and a Polaris jacket beams as the DNR workers hoist a four-foot frozen sturgeon up onto the scale.

"That's my first in twelve years," the spearer proudly declares. Implicit in his statement is twelve seasons spent staring into a hole in the ice, straining to see a long, dark shadow and seeing nothing. Twelve years of sitting in the dark, dangling decoys, waiting. And twelve years isn't even a long time for some other spearers. It's this type of devotion and perseverance that makes this population of fish, above all other creatures in the state's boundaries, a rare gem—one that is envied and eyed the world over. And Ron Bruch is only one of many in Wisconsin working diligently to safeguard it.

There are twenty-seven species of sturgeon worldwide, and all of them are found in the waters of the Northern Hemisphere. Most live primarily in the sea, migrating into freshwater to spawn. Out of eight species in North America only three—the pallid, shovelnose, and lake sturgeon—spend their entire lives in freshwater. All of the species are threatened or endangered in some portion of their original ranges.

Despite their low numbers today, sturgeon are survivors. According to fossil records, they have been on Earth for at least one hundred fifty million years. Dinosaurs died off, glaciers melted, and volcanoes blew their tops, but sturgeon continued to swim and spawn in our oceans, lakes, and rivers, even when those very bodies of water underwent enormous change. Lake sturgeon evolved originally in the Mississippi River. When a glacier melted about fourteen thousand years ago, it left behind the Great Lakes and a new home for lake sturgeon. And, up until recent times, they've done quite well in both places.[1]

To look at a sturgeon is to gaze back at an ancient world. They have remained essentially unchanged for millions of years, and several of their unique features hearken back to the early evolution of fish. A sturgeon's tail fin is sharklike, with an upper lobe longer than the lower lobe. It looks like a scythe cutting through wheat as the fish carve their way through shallow water. Also like sharks, a sturgeon's skeleton is made out of cartilage, the same type of connective tissue as that in the human ear and nose. The backbone is actually a notochord, similar to that of a hagfish or lamprey, and a precursor to the intricate bony column that is filleted out of most fish caught today. Unlike modern fish, sturgeon lack scales. Instead, their skin is tough and thick, topped off with pinched bits of bone called scutes. Five rows of scutes encircle the torpedo-shaped midsection, and a young sturgeon writhing around in your hands can leave painful cuts behind.

Don Burg (right) and his brother Ben from Stockbridge, on the east side of Lake Winnebago, remember their great-uncle's stories of spearing sturgeon with the Stockbridge Indians, a community of Mohican Indians who were relocated from the eastern United States to Wisconsin in the 1820s. The tribe was later moved again in the 1850s to land adjoining the Menominee reservation. When he was young, Ben Burg purchased this decoy for two and a half dollars from Frank Denslow, a Stockbridge Indian who still lived in the area.

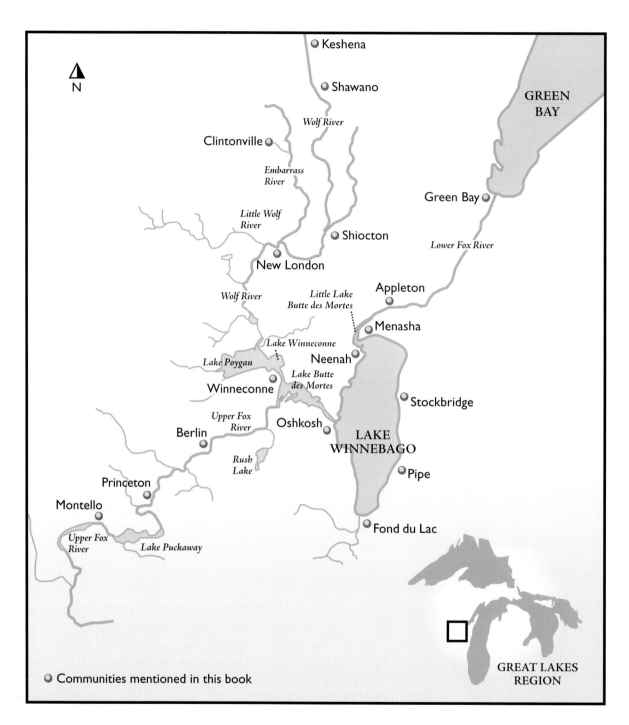

This map may help orient the reader by pinpointing communities and geographic features of the Lake Winnebago System. The Wolf River empties into Lake Poygan. Like many major river systems in Wisconsin, it flows in a southerly direction. The Fox River, however, flows in a northeasterly direction, ultimately feeding into Green Bay and Lake Michigan.

For a long time scientists thought the juvenile and adult lake sturgeon were two different species, and looking at both side by side, it's no wonder. One could say that lake sturgeon "soften" as they age. While a juvenile lake sturgeon has a long, pointy snout, the head of an adult is short and rounded, almost as if it gently eroded away from decades of currents and waves. As the largest fish swimming around in their freshwater homes, they find few predators to contend with once they reach a certain age and size. The sharp, protective scutes dull as they stretch out from years of growth, and the color of the back darkens from a light brown to a murky gray-brown, the same hue as the sediment they cruise above. (Interestingly, ocean-living sturgeon, definitely not the biggest fish in the pond, keep their pronounced scutes throughout their lives.)

Lake sturgeon are bottom dwellers. As they swim close to the bottom of the lake or riverbed, they use their barbels—four "whiskers" at the front of the snout—to feel around for food. Once a sturgeon locates something of interest, it extends a wide, rubbery, tube-like appendage of its mouth and sucks up the food like a powerful vacuum cleaner. Sturgeon primarily stuff themselves on insects such as lakefly larvae, small crustaceans, and clams. But, just like vacuum cleaners, they aren't too picky about what they suck up. Researchers have often slit open a fish's stomach to find it filled with sturgeon eggs.

In the spring, the continuous search for food comes to a halt for some love-struck sturgeon, as warmer water temperatures trigger an ancient migration and mating ritual. Somewhat like salmon, males and females swim up the river of their birth to find rocky substrate for spawning. Fertilized eggs need plenty of oxygen to survive, so spawning in shallow, rushing water is crucial. In fact, it's so important that the fish will, literally, go to great lengths to find the perfect spawning site—some travel as much as 140 miles across Lake Winnebago and up the Wolf River. In the Great Lakes, a sturgeon that was tagged in southern Lake Huron turned up a few years later near Door County, Wisconsin, a distance of roughly five hundred miles.[2] However, after all that searching for the right spot, no more than one out of every fifty thousand of the eggs released by a female is likely to survive and grow into an adult.

Sturgeon reproduction seems like a wasteful crapshoot—a female expends the energy to produce up to a half million eggs, only to add a handful of progeny to the next generation—but it's a gamble that has paid off for a long, long time. However, more recently, it's those hundreds of thousands of eggs—sometimes

For a long time, scientists thought juvenile and adult lake sturgeon were two different species. While a juvenile lake sturgeon (top) has a long, pointy snout, the head of an adult (bottom) is short and round.

GIDDYAP

Although the fish in this story are probably Atlantic sturgeon, it's likely that similar schemes were hatched using lake sturgeon in Lake Winnebago, especially after this piece ran in an 1871 issue of the *Wisconsin State Journal*.

A correspondent of the New York Citizen writing from Easton, Pa., tells the following remarkable fish story:

Two of our distinguished citizens, Mr. Samuel Phillippi and Col. J.R. Sitgreaves, have for many years entertained the notion that sturgeon might be so managed as to draw a pleasure boat. For the last three summers they have been making experiments to solve the problem, and at last have succeeded. The mode of procedure has been every spring when the sturgeons have made their way up the Delaware as high as Bristol, to buy a pair, and towing them behind a boat on the Lehigh canal, so bring them to Lehigh dam, where these gentlemen have a boat house, and a pond enclosed for their aquatic ponies.

The mode of harnessing the sturgeons is peculiar. A broad India rubber band encircling each fish just behind the pectoral fin has a brass ring attached on top. Through these rings a stout ashen pole about eight feet long is inserted, and to two staples in the pole the braces are fastened. There is also a narrow gum elastic band around each sturgeon, just behind the dorsal fin, with a loop in the side holding the opposite ends of a much slighter, to compel them to swim at a regular distance from each other.

Mr. Phillippi, who acts as driver, has his seat in the bow and directs their course with a goad, which is a long pole as thick as one's wrist, with a sharp spike sticking out at right angles from the end, and it is surprising with what alacrity they obey. When they are to be turned to the right or left, a sudden prick on the opposite side of each sturgeon causes the pair to take the desired course. When a greater speed is desired they are pierced near the tail; when they are required to halt the goad is cached [pushed] forward, and they are pricked in front of the head.

There was much difficulty at first in preventing the fish from seeking the bottom and drawing the boat under. They were consequently driven in water not over four feet deep.

Dr. Slack, however, an eminent fish-culturist in the neighborhood, who had traveled in Egypt and had observed the mode of managing sturgeon attached to boats on the Nile, overcame the difficulty. He had two large hollow floats made in the shape of swans, and painted white to resemble those birds. To each of these floats a cord of three feet was attached and fastened into the rings of the pole to which the braces are made fast; the wooden swans thus serving an ornamental as well as a useful purpose. To create the delusion that the boat is drawn by swans, a pair of gay reins reach from the bird-like floats to the bow. The boat is shaped like a shell, and Col. Sitgreaves, sitting in the stern with his trident, which he frequently carries, is no bad representation of Neptune. His Palindras, Sammy Phillippi, who keeps a fast team, is as skillful in directing the course of the aqueous steeds as he is in driving his pair on the road.

It will thus be seen that the piscaculture will not only increase our supply of animal food, but that we may eventually use the larger denizens of the water for purposes of locomotion.

Wisconsin State Journal, July 11, 1871

up to sixty pounds' worth in a large, fertile female—meant to ensure the future of the species, that have led to its demise. Screened and salted, these small round globs of goo become caviar, one of the most coveted delicacies in the world.

But long before their eggs were packaged for sale to restaurants and cruise ships, lake sturgeon lived in relative peace with the Indian tribes in the Great Lakes region. To be sure, every time the fish congregated to spawn, they were netted, and every winter they were speared through the ice. But with eleven million fish estimated to have been living in Lake Michigan alone at that time, there were plenty to go around.[3] In many ways, sturgeon were for Great Lakes tribes what buffalo were to the Great Plains Indians. Both revered and hunted, the fish provided a stable supply of protein, especially in the spring when larders were low after long, harsh winters. Sturgeon probably kept many tribes from starving, and their scutes were sometimes used in medicines.

However, early European settlers were not eager to cook up what they viewed as a gnarly, mud-sucking fish. Settlers at Jamestown paid little notice to the hoards of Atlantic sturgeon spawning in the James River until fear of starvation sent them into the water armed with frying pans and swords. Nearly two hundred years later, a traveler reported seeing all kinds of fish in the Niagara River, close to where it empties into Lake Ontario, including the lake sturgeon, "which is a bad, useless sort of fish."[4] As Europeans continued to press westward, the sturgeon's reputation moved from disgusting to despised. Their sharp scutes sliced through fishing nets, and rumors spread that sturgeon feasted on the eggs of other fish, particularly those of prized commercial species such as whitefish and trout.[5] Seen as both a nuisance and a menace, lake sturgeon were clubbed to death, burned for fuel, and plowed into fields as compost, and occasionally fishermen would wound a few before letting them go, hoping that the bloody water would keep others away.[6]

It's important to keep in mind that lake sturgeon live a long time—up to one hundred years or more, meaning there could be a sturgeon swimming in Lake Winnebago that felt the reverberations of the first Harley-Davidson motorcycle rumbling out of Milwaukee. With such a long time to muck around, these fish don't rush into much. Females are twenty-one to thirty-nine years old before they first spawn, an event they repeat only once every three to five years. Their longevity actually gives lake sturgeon an edge in dealing with some environmental changes, because they can often ride out times when conditions aren't good for reproducing.

Mystery of the Flying Fish

Because lake sturgeon are bottom dwellers, it's somewhat surprising to see one leap clear out of the water. And if the sight of a hundred-pound fish launching itself into the air doesn't impress you, the sound of it crashing back down to the water's surface will cause you to pause (or perhaps take cover, especially if one lands near your boat).

All sturgeon species are known to exhibit this behavior, and scientists aren't sure why. A group of Florida researches have proposed one idea: perhaps leaping is a form of communication. They found that in the Suwannee River—where airborne Gulf sturgeon have been known to physically injure boaters—most of the jumping occurs in the summer, when sturgeon are conserving energy in a few cool-water refuges. They noted that jumping produces a unique acoustic signal, especially as the fish lands in the water flat on its side. The resulting sound can be heard more than half a mile away and probably even farther underwater.[1] In the dark, murky world they inhabit, perhaps sturgeon leap to keep in touch with each other as a group. A loud smack on the water might mean, "Hey, check it out—I found a good spot to hang out!"

NOTE

1. K.J. Sulak et al., "Why Do Sturgeons Jump? Insights from Acoustic Investigations of the Gulf Sturgeon in the Suwannee River, Florida, USA," *J. Appl. Ichthyol* 18 (2002): 617–620.

John Cobb, a field agent for the U.S. Commission of Fish and Fisheries, took this photo of an Atlantic sturgeon landed at the wharf at Caviar, (known today as Bayside) New Jersey, around 1896–1900.

However, their slowness to mature makes it difficult for sturgeon to recover from permanent changes in the environment, much less a direct assault on the population.

Despite surviving whatever killed off the dinosaurs, sturgeon are struggling to endure the effects of a species that, evolutionarily speaking, has existed only a very short time. Over the past 150 years, humans have assaulted the fish in both indirect and direct ways. Lumber mills spewed sawdust into waterways, covering the nooks and crannies where sturgeon love to spawn—those secret little places where eggs can adhere and safely hide out until hatching. But soon, they weren't even able to reach those favorite spawning places, because dams blocked them from swimming upriver in the spring. So by the mid-1800s, sturgeon were having a tough time finding good places to deposit their next generation.

Then, a few enterprising German immigrants made things even tougher by removing that next generation altogether. The advent of railroads and packing ice had brought caviar, the highly perishable Russian delicacy, to Europe, where by the late 1800s it was all the rage among the new bourgeoisie seeking out all things exotic. By then, European sturgeon stocks were virtually fished out, and caviar dealers were searching for a new source. Hearing stories of American rivers teeming with sturgeon, German caviar exporters quickly sent representatives abroad to find out for themselves.

On the East Coast, they first discovered the Delaware River, where fishermen had long lamented that it was impossible not to catch Atlantic sturgeon in their nets. Sturgeon were everywhere—recent immigrants in New York ate the cheap meat and nicknamed it "Albany beef," while salty caviar was served at taverns to encourage heavy drinking. Reports—and samples—sent back to Germany launched a black gold rush, a fishy version of the mining frenzy at Sutter Creek just a few decades before. The fishing port of Caviar, New Jersey, sprung up almost overnight on the shores of the Delaware River. Although hardly a town— during the fishing season it consisted of a store, post office, train station, and about four hundred fishermen living in cabins and houseboats—it soon began sending fifteen train cars of its namesake delicacy off to New York City every day.[7] The finest went to Europe, where it was relabeled Russian caviar and sold for a tidy profit. The rest went to domestic markets, where suddenly there were more orders than could be filled.

The intense demand sent entrepreneurs running to get their hands on a seemingly plentiful commodity. It wasn't long before they set their sights on the

THE RIVER WAS ALIVE WITH STURGEON

Albert C. Weber was born in Shawano, Wisconsin, in 1871. After graduating from high school, he worked as a lumberjack for three years driving logs down the Wolf River. He was the local surveyor as the railroad was built, and he later went on to own lumber and canning businesses in Shawano. A 1924 biography asserts: "[N]o man in the state is perhaps more thoroughly informed on conditions in northern Wisconsin than Mr. Weber, who has done much traveling in that section of the state."[1] He enjoyed hunting and fishing, and later in his life he took a keen interest in local history, making presentations at historical societies and rotary clubs. Here he recounts to a *Shawano County Journal* reporter in 1931 his childhood memories of how the Menominee Indians speared for sturgeon in the spring.

Where the Shawano Hospital now stands was once the main sturgeon ground for the Menominee Indians. When Albert Weber was a little boy, he used to fish with the Indians and he remembers the great sport he had as though it were yesterday. To the little boy it was sport, but to the Indians it was business, a matter of getting food supply for the whole tribe.

The land at the present hospital site presented a long stretch of clean flat sand, covered with pine and young oaks. Every year, when the sturgeon started to run, Indian scouts were sent out to observe their coming, and then a day was appointed for the beginning of sturgeon spearing.

When the day came, the Indians arrived with their canoes, all dug-out canoes made from pine logs and some of them were beauties. The canoes were stacked up on the bank of the river and brush was thrown over them to keep the wood from checking. Usually there were from ninety to a hundred canoes in the pile.

There were two islands out in the middle of the river, where the water was shallow, the channel running this side of the islands. These islands were the accepted mark for starting the sturgeon drive.

Ten or twelve Indians were sent up to the mouth of the Red River. All the others remained at the sturgeon ground. Two or three rows of canoes were stretched across the river to await the sturgeon drive. The fellows who had gone up the river whipped the stream with their spear poles and pretty soon the river was alive with sturgeon. Mr. Weber says that no one can imagine how many there were, so thick in the river that they glommed over each other.

The Indians speared thousands of them during the appointed weeks, not hundreds, but thousands of them. They worked as a sort of community, all sharing alike. On the shore the squaws built up racks like those used for jerking venison and they prepared the fish. The sturgeon were dressed, washed and cut into convenient pieces. The meat was put up onto the racks and were [sic] smoked, cooked a little and dried some and the result was smoked sturgeon which would keep for a long time.

Albert played along with the Indians during that week. His parents did not like sturgeon and forbade him to bring one home, but once in a while, when he got a particularly big prize, he hauled it home through the sand, and invariably got a licking for his pains.

Shawano County Journal, April 30, 1931

NOTE

1. *Wisconsin: Its History and Its People 1634–1924* Volume III (Chicago: The S. J. Clarke Publishing Company, 1924), 322–325.

Great Lakes, where nuisance lake sturgeon were still being fed to pigs and burned as fuel for steamships. Word soon spread that lake sturgeon produced some of the finest caviar of all the species in North America. In 1865, Siemen and John Schacht, German immigrant brothers who had fished on the Delaware River, started a sturgeon-processing plant in Sandusky, Ohio, on the shores of Lake Erie. By 1872, the Schacht brothers were processing more than thirteen thousand fish a year, totaling almost seven hundred thousand pounds' worth. They sold smoked sturgeon, caviar, and isinglass (a type of gelatin clarifying agent made from the fish's swim bladder) to markets all over the world.

James Milner, Great Lakes deputy commissioner for the U.S. Commission of Fish and Fisheries, surveyed the Great Lakes fisheries in 1871 and 1872. In his report, he cheered the success and industriousness of the Schacht brothers, who had arrived in Sandusky only a few years earlier with little money. "Out of a shameful waste of a large supply of food they have established a large and profitable industry," he wrote. Milner wrote disapprovingly about the waste of sturgeon in other communities, especially in Green Bay, Wisconsin, where he saw the fish "useless destroyed or sold by the wagon-load for a trifle."[8] He recommended that other people with ambition follow the Schachts' lead.

Regrettably, too many people did. Great Lakes sturgeon production fell from 7.84 million pounds in 1879 to 1.77 million pounds by 1899.[9] By the time Hugh M. Smith, the next fisheries commissioner, returned to the area in 1913, he was compelled to include a brief account in his report entitled "The Passing of the Sturgeon":

> *The story of the sturgeons is one of the most distressing in the whole history of the American fisheries. These large, inoffensive fishes of our seaboards, coast rivers, and interior waters were for years considered to be not only valueless but nuisances, and whenever they became entangled in the fishermen's nets they were knocked in the head or otherwise mortally wounded and thrown back into the water. . . .*

> *The next chapter in the story was the awakening of the fishermen to the fact that the eggs of the sturgeons had value as caviar and that the flesh had value as food. Then followed the most reckless, senseless fishing imaginable, with the result that in a comparatively few years the best and most productive*

SPLISH SPLASHIN'

Newcomb Spoor was born in Oswego, New York, in 1852. Five weeks later, his family packed up and moved to Wisconsin, where they settled on the north bank of the Fox River, one mile north of the city of Berlin. A "machinist by trade and a farmer by occupation," Spoor also served several years in the Wisconsin state legislature representing Green Lake and Waushara counties.[1] In 1919, he was asked to write an account of sturgeon fishing for a new magazine published by Wisconsin's Conservation Commission, later to become the Department of Natural Resources.

Five men who were active in the Progressive movement stand in front of the *Capitol Times* building in Madison in 1931. Newcomb Spoor stands in the center.

This string of lakes with the Fox and Wolf rivers with their tributaries made it the ideal fishing spot of the world. Almost all kinds of fresh water fish were found in abundance and there being no protection they were speared, netted, snagged and trapped. These fish were hauled to the fields for fertilizer and fed to hogs. In the spring of 1856 a float bridge was built across the Fox river at our home, it floated on the water. The sturgeon usually made their run up the Fox and Wolf rivers in the first or second week in May. During these few days of their run you could see these fish six or seven feet long run up out of the water their full length and fall in again with a huge splash, sometimes three or four at a time, during this time it was not safe to sit on the railing of the bridge unless you wanted to get soaked. One big fish following another would lunge out of the water and falling back would splash the water clear across the bridge and in the morning the planks looked as if it had rained all night. Horses were frightened and runaways were common.

Wisconsin Conservationist, May 1919

NOTE

1. *Wisconsin Blue Book*, 1923, 624, http://digital.library.wisc.edu/1711.dl/WI.WIBlueBks.

waters were depleted, and what should have been made a permanent fishery of great profit was destroyed. Even after the great value of the sturgeon began to be appreciated by every one, the immature and unmarketable fish incidentally caught in seines, gill nets, and pound nets received no protection whatever in most waters and were ruthlessly destroyed as nuisances, the decline being thus doubly accelerated.

Everywhere in America, under existing conditions, the sturgeons are doomed to commercial extinction, and it requires no prophet to foretell that in a comparatively few years the sturgeon will be practically extinct. What is demanded in every State in which these fishes exist or have existed is absolute prohibition of capture or sale for a long term of years, certainly not less than 10. To advocate any less radical treatment would be only trifling with the situation.[10]

Fortunately, one state took serious note of Smith's predictions. Actually, its fisheries managers already had made the same forecast. Ten years earlier, in 1903, Wisconsin had enacted a closed spring season on sturgeon in the Lake Winnebago System, and by 1915 a statewide moratorium on sturgeon fishing went on the books. It remained to be seen if it was too late to make any difference.

This photo of a large sturgeon was taken near Fond du Lac in 1915, the same year that a statewide moratorium on sturgeon fishing went into effect in Wisconsin. Linus Venne, eight years old, is standing on the far left. The boy standing to the right of the sturgeon is John Moral, also eight years old.

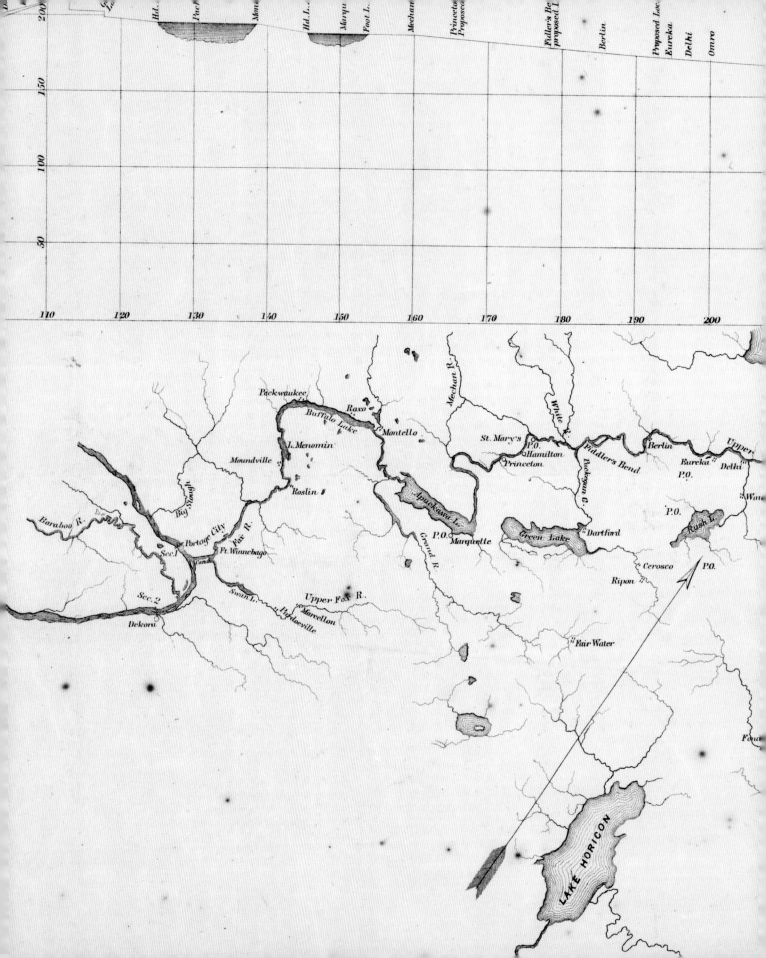

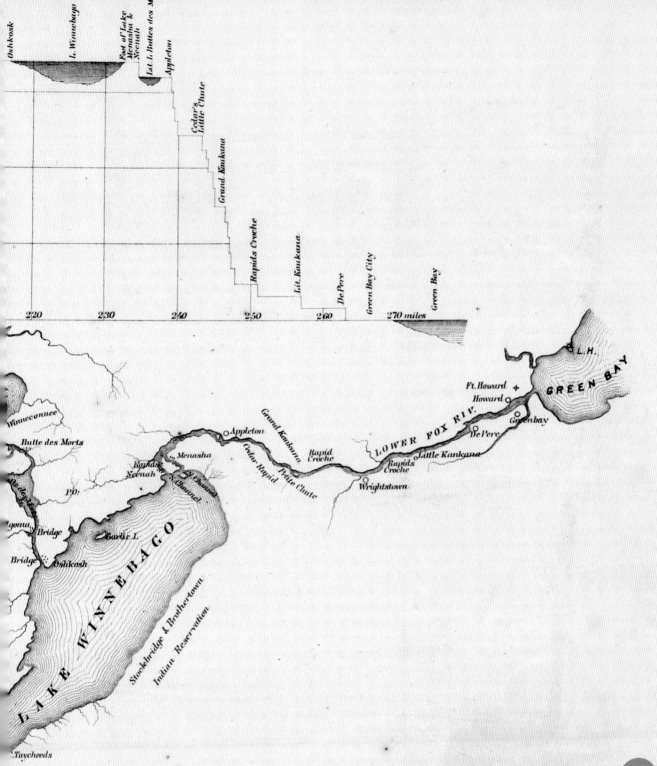

Oshkosk
I. Winnebago
Foot of Lake
Menasha &
Neenah
Lit. I. Buttes des Mo
Appleton
Cedar's
Little Chute
Grand Kaukana
Rapids Croche
Lit. Kaukana
DePere
Green Bay City
Green Bay

220   230   240   250   260   270 miles

G.L.H.
GREEN BAY
Ft. Howard
Howard
Greenbay
De Pere
Little Kaukana
LOWER FOX RIV.
Grand Kaukana
Rapid
Croche
Rapids
Croche
Wrightstown
Petite Chute
Cedar Rapid
Winneconnee
Butte des Morts
Menasha
Rapids
Neenah
S. Channel
St. Theunius
P.O.
goma
Bridge
Garlic I.
Bridge   Oshkosh
LAKE WINNEBAGO
Stockbridge & Brothertown
Indian Reservation
Tayckeds

FISH LAWS 2

By the time people in Wisconsin started turning their attention to lake sturgeon in the early 1900s, the fish had nearly disappeared from the Great Lakes due to overfishing, dams, and pollution. Although numbers had also declined in Lake Winnebago, Wisconsin's largest inland lake, the situation wasn't quite as dire, and the reason had much to do with location.

First, the Great Lakes experienced intense commercial fishing, yet this had no effect on the Lake Winnebago population of sturgeon. Winnebago sturgeon, while considered a Great Lakes strain, have always been a separate, distinct population from the rest of the sturgeon living in the Lake Michigan watershed, separated by a geographic barrier—the Lower Fox River.

Historically, sturgeon living in Green Bay and Lake Michigan traveled up the Lower Fox to spawn, and it wasn't an easy journey. On its way from Lake Winnebago to where it empties into Green Bay thirty-nine miles downstream, the Lower Fox drops 170 feet—nearly the height of Niagara Falls. Significant rapids and ample spawning sites probably kept most Lake Michigan sturgeon from ever bothering to push all the way up to Lake Winnebago. And since 1856, when an ambitious construction project was launched to link the Great Lakes and the Mississippi River, fourteen dams and seventeen locks have made the journey impossible.

In 1893 the state legislature approved five thousand dollars to buy a railcar specifically designed for transporting and stocking fish around Wisconsin. Named Badger, the car held twelve fish tanks, each three feet square and eighteen inches deep. Badger made an impressive debut that year at the World's Columbian Exposition in Chicago, where it delivered a large collection of live native fish, including lake sturgeon, to be displayed in an aquarium at the Fisheries Building.

Previous page: This 1867 map by the U.S. Corps of Engineers shows the significant vertical drop (170 feet) between Lake Winnebago and Green Bay. In 1856, a system of locks and dams was constructed on the Lower Fox River in an effort to create a viable waterway connecting the Great Lakes to the Mississippi River.

While Lake Michigan sturgeon weren't able to make it all the way upstream, Winnebago sturgeon had little need to make the fast and furious trip down to Green Bay. Lake Winnebago is an ideal home for adult lake sturgeon—wide, shallow, and full of things to eat; the smaller "Upriver Lakes" (Butte des Morts, Winneconne, and Poygan) serve as nurseries for juveniles; and in the spring, spawning sturgeon search out rocky upstream areas of the Wolf, Embarrass, and Upper Fox rivers.[1]

The location of these rivers meant that the Winnebago sturgeon didn't suffer another blow that doomed so many Great Lakes sturgeon—loss of spawning sites because of dams and pollution. Spawning sturgeon prefer clean, rocky shorelines with swift-moving water. While many rivers feeding into the Great Lakes were dammed for hydroelectric power or polluted by various industries, the rivers feeding Lake Winnebago remained relatively clean and free flowing because they ran through thick pine forests that fueled the state's first major industry.

Lumbermen considered the Wolf River one of the best waterways in the Great Lakes states for driving logs; it had relatively few rapids on its lower section and many tributaries that reached into some of the finest pine forests in the state. Because the river was so conducive to driving logs, the timber was floated downriver to Oshkosh, home to more than forty steam-driven mills (in contrast to other rivers in the state, where mills were constructed right along the rivers and powered by dams).[2] Much of the Little Wolf, Embarrass, and Upper Fox stayed relatively open as well. Not only did more than two hundred miles of river continue to provide open access to spawning habitat for the Winnebago sturgeon, these rivers stayed relatively free of sawdust, which could smother the shallow, rocky areas where sturgeon prefer to deposit their eggs. Instead, the sawdust was concentrated in Oshkosh, where it was used primarily as fill along the Fox River through the city.[3]

Location also gave the new state conservation department a unique opportunity to manage the sturgeon in the Lake Winnebago system. Unlike the lake sturgeon populations in other parts of the Great Lakes watershed and Mississippi River, the Winnebago fishery was entirely within one state's borders. Any regulations Wisconsin enacted would affect the entire fishery, without the need to coordinate with another state or federal agency. It was a golden opportunity, but it certainly wasn't going to be easy.

"There isn't a single natural resource in the state of Wisconsin that the people wouldn't utterly destroy if they weren't curtailed. They've done so with the pine, and the homing pigeon, and with every other thing that they have been unrestricted to control and to operate. If it wasn't for the control of the fishing program . . . there wouldn't be a darn fish left."

—Brayton O. Webster, Wisconsin Superintendent of Fisheries, 1923–1944 [4]

Opposite page: Men spear sturgeon on the Wisconsin River at the dam in Kilbourn, a town that was renamed Wisconsin Dells in 1931.

The photograph was taken by H. H. Bennett (1843–1908)

The rapid decline of all types of fish is what first drove Wisconsin's state government into the wildlife-management business. The first Fisheries Commission was organized in 1874 to survey the status of fisheries throughout the state, but its most pressing task was to build fish hatcheries. The idea was that if there weren't enough fish to go around, the state should raise more and plant them in the waterways.

However, in surveying the state's waters, it became clear that stocking alone wouldn't solve the problem of dwindling fish numbers. In 1879, the state superintendent of fisheries described some of the major threats that needed to be addressed. By far the greatest concern was dams blocking the spawning runs of fish in the spring. Not only were the fish prevented from moving upriver to their spawning grounds, they were easy targets for fishermen as they congregated at the foot of the dam. Unable to continue their travels, many of these fish were slaughtered by what the superintendent called the "nefarious practice" of spearing.[5] He appealed to the legislature for "stringent laws and a better enforcement of them than we have had, in the direction of protecting fish from wanton spoliation, as well as protection by giving to the fish the free use of the waters, in which they were originally placed by a beneficent Providence."[6]

Prior to the creation of the Commission of Fisheries, fishing had been regulated on a county basis, and most people were oblivious to any rules governing how many or what kind of fish could be taken out of any particular body of water. One of the first steps the commission took was to record all of the fish laws in one document. But even though this small step was merely administrative, it was met with animosity. When the commissioners brought the document to the legislature for approval, so many conflicting local interests were stirred up that the bill was defeated.[7] Apparently, fish laws were—and would continue to be—a touchy subject in Wisconsin.

Two boys stand among stumps in northern Wisconsin cutover land. The photograph was taken in 1937, but the trees had been cut down forty years earlier by loggers. The cheap, barren land left behind attracted many immigrants to northern Wisconsin in the early twentieth century.

Slowly, the commission was able to secure the legislature's approval for a handful of regulations—and spears were one of the first things to go. But as more restrictions were created, certain areas of the state began pushing for special exemptions. The most outspoken areas were along the Mississippi River, Green Bay, and Lake Winnebago—regions settled by French explorers in the 1600s, where the pioneer dependence on subsistence fishing and hunting was especially strong and ingrained. Apparently, people in these regions, especially those living along Lake Winnebago, were also very good at making their feelings known to their legislators. By 1887, spears were made legal for sturgeon in the waters of Lake Winnebago and the Fox and Wolf rivers.[8] In 1892, when all types of nets were illegal in most Wisconsin inland waters, gill nets were still allowed in the Lake Winnebago system.[9] And while ice shanties were nearly outlawed throughout the state in 1897, two years later Lake Winnebago had secured an exemption.[10] Outspoken residents of the region would eventually be known to state officials, in polite terms, as a "well organized and noisy group."[11] However, to many of the growing number of conservationists in the state, they were known simply as "fish hogs."

As some people fought to maintain the old ways of life with unlimited access to fish and game, others were pushing forward new ways to manage dwindling resources in the midst of expanding populations of people. The Progressive Republicans, led by Robert La Follette Sr., advocated for stronger conservation policies, as did private groups such as the Izaak Walton League. Some of the university faculty joined in the movement as well—University of Wisconsin president Charles Van Hise, a noted geologist, provided conservation advice to Theodore Roosevelt and also wrote the first U.S. textbook on conservation in 1910.[12]

By the turn of the century, lumberjacks had stripped northern Wisconsin of its thick pine forests, leaving behind millions of acres of barren land littered with tree stumps.[13] Buffalo hadn't been seen in the southern part of the state since 1830.[14] Perhaps with the death of the last passenger pigeon in 1914, marking the extinction of a species that once darkened Wisconsin skies with its abundance, legislators finally decided to take action. In 1915, a major overhaul of conservation happened in Wisconsin, rolling the Fisheries Commission into a new Conservation Commission that would oversee all facets of forestry and wildlife management. As part of the many changes, the legislature enacted a ban on all sturgeon harvest. People hoped that by protecting the fish it would have time to repopulate. However, it would take far more than a new law on the books to fully protect sturgeon.

Wisconsin wardens Emil Kramer and Glenn Popple examine illegal catches of sturgeon in 1935.

The Law Says No

"A big fat sturgeon was seen rubbing his back against one of the pilings just below the Huron street bridge Monday afternoon. It was about nine feet long and looked as though he'd make good feed. But the law says no."
—*Oshkosh Daily Northwestern*, May 11, 1916

Despite the ban on sturgeon, arrests for poaching, particularly of residents living along the Wolf River, showed up frequently in the newspapers in the spring when sturgeon began their spawning run upriver. "There is unquestionably very much 'hogging' of the fish supply," said William Mauthe, chairman of the Conservation Commission, in a speech made in Fond du Lac. "Illegal fishing on the Wolf is so well known that it is a common thing for a fish hog to be dubbed a 'Winneconne sportsman,'" referring to the small town straddling the Wolf River between Lake Winneconne and Lake Butte des Morts.[15]

Many of the poachers who were caught simply paid the fines, but some pled not guilty and often presented barefaced explanations. After Game Warden I. H. Boomer caught George Lonkey with sturgeon in Shiocton, Lonkey's defense was that he "did not know how the fish happened to be in his car."[16] Along the same line, Theodore Korn of Winneconne, after being charged by Deputy Game Warden W. A. Keys for possessing sturgeon, filed the defense "that if sturgeon was found in the ice box at Mr. Korn's place, as alleged, it was placed there without his knowledge by some person unknown to him."[17]

On the river, the easiest way to catch sturgeon was to stretch a line across the water and hang a series of large, barbed hooks from it. These unbaited "snag lines" simply relied on sturgeon running into and getting caught on the hooks. In the early spring, the snag lines were weighted with lead to hang close to the river bottom as the sturgeon made their way upriver to spawn. But the best time to catch them was after the spawning run, when the exhausted fish simply float downstream headfirst, letting the water propel them, steering with their pectoral fins. To catch these sturgeon, the hooks were weighted to hang closer to the water's surface.

Downstream, in the Upriver Lakes and Lake Winnebago where there was no strong current, a different method was used. "Setlines" were baited fishing lines weighted down in the water, some containing hundreds of hooks. They were—and still are—legal for catching catfish, but they were very efficient at hooking sturgeon, too.

Ed Gorchals of Larsen, Wisconsin, remembers being arrested for using setlines one night fifty years ago. "They took my boat and motor and my license for the year, put me in jail for three days . . . so I paid for it," he said. When asked why he took the risk, Gorchals said it was simple: "We needed the money."

Warden Emil Kramer and his assistant remove an illegal snag line from the Wolf River near Shiocton in 1942.

To hook a single sturgeon, fishermen used treble hooks strung to fishing poles or simple handlines.

Left: Snag lines—weighted with lead and with hooks suspended at various depths in the water column—often caught many fish at a time, as fish moved upstream and downstream.

HIDDEN TREASURE

Robert "Jake" Abraham was born in 1921 and has lived his whole life in the same spot on the west shore of Lake Winnebago, just across the road from the tavern Wendt's on the Lake. Growing up he helped out on the family farm, and he began working as a duck-hunting guide in 1943, eventually guiding for men like former Wisconsin governor Warren Knowles and Augie Pabst from the famous Milwaukee brewery family.

Abraham remembers "running" setlines on Lake Winnebago in the 1930s with his dad and brother. "That's how we made extra money," he said. "There was no money in farming."

One year, when Abraham was about nine years old, the duck hunting was poor and the lakes stayed clear of ice late into the season. His dad and another man from Oshkosh decided to focus their efforts on setlines, and they managed to place nine hundred hooks in the water. However, the lake froze over before they could pull the setlines out. So they put a boat on a sleigh and headed out on the ice to retrieve their lines.

Abraham said they had to hunt around a bit for the setlines because they were hidden by a few inches of ice. "So they cut some holes and took a stick about twenty feet long with a drag on it," he said. "They didn't go very far; they had a line . . . and they pulled out thirty-two sturgeon on that line."

"They brought them all home, and they were out there all day. My mother and sister, they thought they drowned out there. They didn't come home until after dark. . . . And finally they came. They had broken through with the boat a couple of times, but they wouldn't let go of them sturgeon."

The sturgeon ranged from thirty to eighty pounds, and the men caught a total of a 134 that fall. "I don't have any pictures of them," Abraham said. "I wish I did."

While many stolen sturgeon were simply eaten at family dinner tables or sold for some extra spending money, others fueled a profitable commercial business that extended outside of the state. An Oshkosh man, Lee Ogden, was arrested after wardens discovered his elaborate scheme of shipping sturgeon and other game fish to Chicago in trunks checked through as regular baggage. The baggage claim checks were sent by mail to the Lakeside Fish and Oyster Company so that the trunks could be retrieved upon arrival at the train station.[18] Schemes like this were often wrapped up in other illegal activities such as bootlegging, so it's very likely that caviar from Winnebago sturgeon at some point ended up in the mouth of Al Capone, the infamous Chicago gangster.

Lobbying for Sturgeon

As the Great Depression started taking hold of the state's economy, people who remembered enjoying a satisfying meal of smoked sturgeon started to speak up about regaining legal access to the fish.

It started with a few local hunting and fishing clubs, organizations that had been founded in the early 1900s by conservation-minded sportsmen. In addition to maintaining private land for hunting and fishing, many of the clubs organized their own patrols before the state warden system was solidly in place. By the 1930s, with more and more restrictive regulations being placed on hunters and fishers, these local clubs were taking on the additional role of advocating for public access to the resources.

At their monthly meetings at the Danish Brotherhood Hall in Neenah, members of the Twin City Sportsmen's Club began discussing the idea of lobbying the legislature to open a season for spearing sturgeon through the ice. The state had been paying commercial fishermen to remove nuisance "rough" fish like carp from Lake Winnebago, and word had spread that the nets were also bringing up loads of sturgeon. The Twin City club members began rationalizing that if that many sturgeon were in the lake, then surely a recreational spear fishery could be sustained with certain size restrictions and catch limits.[19]

The Blame Game

After sturgeon were officially protected in 1915, people around Lake Winnebago began searching for what—or who—was to blame for the dwindling numbers of sturgeon that the Conservation Commission kept referencing. Some people said the problem was polluted water, others said there were too many carp in the lake eating sturgeon eggs, but a majority of people pointed fingers at the poachers who preyed on spawning sturgeon during the spring.

Wardens did the best they could, but it was impossible to patrol more than two hundred miles of spawning grounds along the Wolf River and its tributaries, especially at night. As far as people living around Lake Winnebago were concerned, their spearing season had been eliminated because of violators on the rivers.

Meanwhile, residents of the small river towns heard reports of state-funded commercial fishermen who were allowed to use nets to remove nuisance fish out of Lake Winnebago. While the operations were supposed to be supervised by wardens, word got around that captured sturgeon weren't always being released back into the water.

After a story entitled "Keep Up Fight on Sturgeon Fishers" ran in an Appleton newspaper, praising some recent prosecutions of river poachers, one resident of Shiocton, a small town on the lower Wolf River, wrote back with a tongue-in-cheek letter to the editor. »

The ban on sturgeon harvest coincided with Prohibition, so poaching and bootlegging often went hand in hand. Here, three fishermen celebrate their catch of sturgeon, catfish, and sheepshead. The photo was likely taken near Tustin on the northwest corner of Lake Poygan.

"If This Be Treason, Make the Most of It"

Appleton Post Crescent, May 7, 1923

Inasmuch as some [of] the respected citizens of our law abiding community have been held up as gross violators of the law, and our fair names have been blemished in a way that hurts our conscience, we, singly and collectively, after a mass meeting, feel that the results of the public sentiment, as well as our view point should be set forth to the people of Outagamie county of which we feel that we constitute no small part.

From ancient times there has always been a survival of the fittest in human life as well as in these modern days of keen commercialism. We wish here to state that no sturgeon ever met his Waterloo from a commercial standpoint. We have endeavored to exterminate the species from entirely a different standpoint. We wish to tell you people of the higher lands the real reason why at times some of us have felt it incumbent to violate the, to us, illegal law. Take for instance such large stock raisers as our worth and respected citizen, Mr. C. W. Singler. He has to spend a large amount of money each year to build a sturgeon proof fence around his farm. This year he has been complaining of the unusual ferocity of the sturgeon. They tore down his fences in several places and he now has several good dairy cows, minus part of their tails, bitten off by these ferocious fish. This causes a large financial loss to their owner as they are worth a deal less without their tails.

We have a very accurate chronological expert, who has been for years the official keeper of the weather forecasts, state of the river flow and from years of experience has developed into a real expert at figures. He not only has put up an idea that will save the tax payers of this county thousands of dollars, but to us, we feel he has solved the problem of how to take care of the damaging waters that every spring cover our fertile lands. The Northern Farms under the able guidance and every watchful care of our worthy citizen Mike Mack spends $15 every 24 hours pumping water which will all be eliminated if we will be permitted by law to put our plan into practicable operation.

It is reported on good authority that every fifteen minutes an average of 377 large sized sturgeon go under our wagon bridge. Think of the vast amount of cubic feet of space these large fish are taking from our river bed, built by nature to be amply large enough to take care of the surplus water, but through the space now used by these fish it is crowding the water over the banks and causing such progressive communities as join this river an annual loss of many thousands of dollars. We feel that we should be privileged to take these fish from the river and then be able to keep the river within its bed and save all the loss it entails each year.

If some of our respected citizens have, after becoming desperate and receiving no redress from their complaints felt upon themselves to do their humble part in helping eliminate the annual menace of the encroaching waters, and should they run afoul of the ever watchful eyes of those elected to protect a few legalized sportsmen that net our sturgeon and pike from the placid waters of Lake Winnebago, we ask that you judge them with leniency as they sure have cause, that we are not pirates, but worthy citizens endeavoring to do what is right according to our light.

We place this before the people of our worthy county and we are content to let you be the judge.

Respectfully yours,

The Citizens of Shiocton,
(Per) B. G. Curtis, Sec.

Governor Philip La Follette (center) with a day's catch on Trout Lake, Vilas County, in 1937. With him are Governor Henry Horner of Illinois (left) and Governor Nelson Kraschel of Iowa.

But it wasn't just the spearers who had their eyes on sturgeon. Residents living around the Upriver Lakes had noticed there were more fish, too, especially in the fall, when sturgeon would move into the small lakes in preparation to spawn the next spring. In early 1931, State Senator Merritt F. White from Winneconne drafted a bill to open sturgeon to a fall hook-and-line season. Soon after, legislators from around Lake Winnebago had amended the bill to include a two-month ice spearing season on the big lake.

The bill passed the assembly by a vote of sixty-eight to seventeen on March 12, 1931. However, Governor Philip F. La Follette vetoed it two weeks later—the first veto of his administration. The reason had to do with the amended season on spearing. "The Conservation Director advises that that portion of this bill which provides an open season for spearing sturgeon through the ice in Lake Winnebago between January 1st and March 1st would be unwise," La Follette explained in a letter to the senate.[20]

Indeed, the conservation director, Paul Kelleter, was firmly against the bill and had accordingly advised the governor to veto it. "The disturbing feature of the proposed legislation," he wrote to La Follette, "is the provision for spearing through the ice from January 1 to March 1." Kelleter worried that spearing sturgeon would gain popularity and "doubtless hasten the complete destruction of sturgeon in Winnebago waters."[21] He added that even with sixteen years of protection, "the sturgeon has not increased in numbers in these waters sufficiently to warrant an open season at this time and the removal of protection as contemplated by the proposed legislation before you is not in the best interests of conservation."[22]

It's unclear exactly what sort of backroom negotiations took place next. The legislature voted unanimously to not override the governor's veto—even Senator White went along with the decision. But the very next day, White introduced another bill, exactly identical to the first. When the assembly's Committee on Conservation met to review the bill, a large contingent of members from the Oshkosh chapter of the Wisconsin Hunting and Fishing Protective Association traveled to Madison to show their support.[23] On May 21, only two people in the assembly voted against it, and La Follette signed it into law the next month.

Clearly the governor had a change of heart, but the reason why is difficult to decipher. His term limit was two years—and after accounting for at least six months of campaigning for the next election, that left only eighteen months to really get anything done. He was planning to call a special session of the legislature

CAT AND MOUSE

KEN CORBETT

Ken Corbett grew up in Chilton, Wisconsin, on the east side of Lake Winnebago, and he got his start as a warden in Clintonville, along the Embarrass River, in 1956. He was the first warden ever stationed there, and he worked hard to make his presence known. "You never know where or when you're gonna run into that guy," said one local river man at the time. "It wouldn't surprise me if I was sitting in my boat in the middle of the river and he popped up out of the water next to me."[1]

Corbett eventually became one of the state's first flying wardens, surveying hunting and fishing activities from the air and working with wardens on the ground to apprehend violators. As such, he had a bird's-eye view of illegal snag line activities happening down below in the river. If new, shiny lead weights were used on the lines, he could see them flicker in the sunlight.

Corbett once arrested a man who was running a fairly sophisticated commercial sturgeon business just south of Shawano. "After I locked him up, he said, 'Corbett, I bet you never saw equipment like that.' All brand new and really nice stuff." Six years later or so, Corbett was flying early in the morning, tracing the river just as the sun was coming up. The home of the violator had a long pier, and Corbett saw little flashes of light in the water. It turned out to be a snag line staked out under the pier, its hooks loaded down with brand-new weights. Apparently old habits die hard.

On the ground, Corbett spent a lot of time working "lay jobs." After locating a snag line, he would hide in the brush and wait for someone to return to the line to check for sturgeon. Sometimes lay jobs turned into days of camping out and waiting. But if he had a good idea of who owned the line, Corbett would turn to one of the evidence-collecting kits provided by the state crime lab in Madison. "There was a powder, a liquid, and a salve that you could put on the equipment, and if they touched it—we had a purple black light—well, that guy would light up like a tavern sign," he said.

While surveying by air, Corbett's plane was often fired at by violators on the river. Luckily, he was usually flying at about seven thousand feet, so the bullets couldn't reach him. But just to be safe, and to calm his wife's worries, he lined the floor of his cockpit with a bunch of old catalogs. And every now and then, he'd buzz down close to the river at night, just to remind the men secretly checking their snag lines that he was around and watching.

Ken Corbett (left) and Haze Diemel Jr. once played games of cat and mouse up and down the Wolf River.

"I would harass them a bit with the landing lights—just terrify the hell out of them, those two big landing lights coming out of the sky," Corbett remembered. "I'd be at about one thousand feet, and they'd look up at those big lights. And it was noisier than hell— I'd make sure it was out of sync." He laughed. "RARARARARARARAR!!! They always talk about that."

HAZE DIEMEL JR.

Haze Diemel Jr. grew up on the Wolf River on a piece of land that has been in his family since 1860. The land was once home to a large village of Meskwaki Indians (also known as the Fox or Outagamie), who came to Wisconsin in the mid-seventeenth century during the Iroquois War. The Meskwaki were known to take sturgeon out of the river, and Diemel did, too.

"There was a lot different attitude than there is now," said Diemel, who helped found the local conservation group Shadows On The Wolf. "If you wanted a sturgeon in those days, you just went and got one. In the fall many years ago, my dad would say, 'Today's the day we're gonna go.' We'd each take a spear, we'd take the flat-bottom boat, we'd go up above to what's called Jake Scott's Red Banks up there, put the boat in, which is about five miles from here, and float back to here. And sooner or later on the way down to here, we'd find a sturgeon on the sand bar, we'd get our fish and go home, and that's it for the year. You get your one fish and he was happy."

In his "violating days," Diemel sold a few sturgeon, but he never made much money. He said it was more about the challenge of trying to get away with it.

One time, Diemel caught a few sturgeon, and he knew of an interested buyer. He went to clean the fish back behind his house—a process that provides an interesting glimpse at the unique biology of sturgeon.

"You cut the tail off, and you cut around the head, but you do not break the backbone," Diemel explained. "Then you twist it, and you pull, and the head will separate from the body. Then you get in there and you grab that cord, and you pull that cord out. And once that spinal cord is pulled out, it'll be almost double the length that it originally was in the fish."

Sturgeon are one of the few freshwater fish swimming around today that still have that cord—known as a notochord by scientists. Lamprey—the only freshwater fish more primitive than sturgeon—also have it. Because of its uniqueness, the cord sometimes draws attention.

"Well, anyway, we went and sold the fish," Diemel continued, "and when we came home, three of my kids were jumping rope with the cords in the front yard. I nearly had a heart attack! So if the wardens went by, they never noticed."

Diemel had a close call with the notochords, but it's clear that he and others in the area had a good time giving the wardens the runaround. One year they ran a "boat factory" in the dance hall of the tavern he owned. They built eight boats that were all identical—sixteen-foot flat-bottom scows, all painted exactly the same.

"That airplane, everyday virtually, would fly the river and try to keep track of all the boats," Diemel said. "So we'd make it a little hard for him. We put boats underneath the bridge where you can't see them from the airplane, or we'd take a boat out into the marsh someplace and just leave it there, for something for him to watch."

Diemel knew the radio frequencies the wardens used, so he could listen in on the confusion that ensued as the pilot, Ken Corbett, tried to direct his team on the ground to one of the boats. "But these boats were all identical, so they were trying to identify them—so it gave them something to do," he said, smiling.

NOTE

1. "Game Warden to Leave Post July 1," *Appleton Post–Crescent*, June 23, 1963, D2.

Metal tags such as these were used to register sturgeon after the legislature and La Follette approved an official spearing season on Lake Winnebago in 1931.

to convene in the fall, with the intention of enacting sweeping unemployment relief as the state's economy sank deeper into the Depression. La Follette, a Progressive Republican, knew he had to play his cards carefully to get the support he needed for his ambitious agenda. "The composition of the Legislature for the 1931 session looked dark," he later wrote in his memoir. "We had firm control of the Assembly; but the Senate, with its four-year term, was controlled by Democrats and Conservative Republicans."[24] Senator White was one of those Conservative Republicans, as were the assemblymen who also backed the bill. Perhaps La Follette decided not to waste any political capital on sturgeon—he had bigger fish to fry.

In any case, it was the beginning of a regulated spearing season in Wisconsin, which would continue into the present day. It was also the start of a search for the right balance between protecting a valuable resource and respecting the cultures surrounding it.

Keep Off the Ice

Spear or no spear, ice fishing in general had become a contentious issue in Wisconsin. Conservationists had been fighting to prohibit it since the 1920s, but the Depression made it difficult to proceed. In 1931 alone, eight bills came before the legislature favoring looser restrictions on ice fishing as economic relief measures. The reasoning was if jobs were nowhere to be found, then at least the unemployed could have a chance to live off the land—or water. However, once the Conservation Commission began regulating fish and game seasons directly (as opposed to legislators representing their district's special interests), the debate on ice fishing really started to heat up.

Overall, the Conservation Commission simply did not like the idea of people out fishing on the ice, landing unknown quantities of fish under the cover of their shanties. And many of the resort owners in Wisconsin felt the same way. Tourism had become increasingly important to the state's economy, and resorts and cabins had sprung up all around lakes and rivers, catering to the wealthy looking for summertime retreats with clean air and good fishing. Conservationists and resort owners blamed ice fishing for depleting the state's inland waters of fish, resulting in diminished spawning runs in the spring and fewer fish for tourists to catch in the summer. On top of that, abandoned, sunken shanties were proving to be dangerous obstacles to the new motorized boats that were becoming popular.

So the commission slowly started restricting ice fishing, first limiting the number of tip-ups per person, then outlawing ice shanties (once again, Lake Winnebago managed to secure an exemption), and finally shortening the season. Its ultimate goal was to achieve uniform regulations for the whole state, eliminating the special exemptions that areas like the Lake Winnebago region had been enjoying for years. "These communities have been privileged for many years and if the privilege is now taken from them, there will, of course, at first be considerable criticism," wrote B.O. Webster, superintendent of fisheries.[25] He would prove to be right on the mark about that.

At the Wisconsin Conservation Congress meeting in July 1938, delegates from all of the counties met to discuss their opinions and offer recommendations for revising fish and game laws. Ice fishing was a hot topic, and sturgeon spearing through the ice got caught up in the debate.

HERON OR HERRING?

Senator Merritt F. White's sturgeon bill that proposed the first regulated spearing season was one of the last fish and game laws passed before a significant shake-up occurred in Wisconsin's management of conservation. In 1933, the authority to regulate fish and game was taken from the legislature and given to the Conservation Commission. It was an action advocated by many conservation organizations, none more than the Izaak Walton League, one of the earliest national conservation organizations in the United States.

Frank Graass, who grew up in Sturgeon Bay, joined the Wisconsin chapter and represented the league at the state capitol in Madison. He had his hands full trying to gain support for conservation measures during what could be called the "Wild West" days of fish and game legislation—when any legislator could propose a bill to change a season or bag limit.

Dick Koerner of Neenah was first elected to the Wisconsin Conservation Congress in 1966, and he has served on it ever since as a representative for Winnebago County. An avid sturgeon spearer for more than fifty years, Koerner has also served on the Winnebago Citizens Sturgeon Advisory Committee since it formed in 1992. Much like the Conservation Congress, the committee provides a voice for sturgeon spearers and other conservation organizations in the management of the Winnebago sturgeon population.

You know, legislators are always good fellows, and sometimes the facts have been mis-represented to them, and often times they will admit that they just don't know what it's all about. . . . A lot of funny things happened. I recall one time the women of Wisconsin put in a bill to protect the blue heron. Well, in commercial fishing, we have a herring, and the senator from Douglas County said to me, "Frank, this blue heron, is that a game fish or a rough fish?"[1]

Graass knew most legislators hadn't the time nor expertise to study the scientific evidence and decide accordingly. A former legislator himself, he knew politicians were always looking for more votes, and a bill that extended a fishing season or increased a catch limit was an easy way to get them. However, these bills started to clog up legislative sessions, and Graass said the logjam ultimately convinced the legislature to abandon fish and game regulation in 1933.

During every session of the legislature, the legislators introduced bills for themselves or at the request of some individuals or group of hunters or fishermen irrespective of the merits of the bill. Every session 1,200 to 1,400 bills were introduced and an average of 200 bills per session related to fish and game. . . . These bills included changing seasons, the methods of hunting and fishing, length of fish, trapping laws, relating to specific counties or county. Consequently, the rules and regulations were so confusing that it almost took a civil engineer or surveyor to tell you where you could hunt and fish and maybe a Philadelphia lawyer to tell you what the law was.[2]

As part of the transfer of regulatory powers, public hearings were instituted to gather public input before the fish and game laws were revised every year by the commission. These public hearings evolved into the Wisconsin Conservation Congress, a group of delegates from each county that met annually to compile recommendations for the Conservation Commission. In 1972, Governor Patrick Lucy signed legislation that legally formed the Wisconsin Conservation Congress, to ensure that citizens would have a voice in state natural resource management.

NOTES

1. Conservation reminiscences of Frank N. Graass, January 28, 1965, SC 972, Wisconsin Historical Society, Madison, WI.
2. Ibid.

O. K. Johnson, a warden from Shawano County, complained that the spearing season on Lake Winnebago made his job of protecting spawning sturgeon on the Wolf River much more difficult. "They spear them until March 15," he told the congress. "Thirty days later they are up in Shawano county. Our boys want to take them. They can't understand what difference it makes whether they take them thirty days later or thirty days earlier. From an enforcement angle, it is impossible to regulate. They will cooperate a lot more if there is no ice fishing on sturgeon."

Howard Leppla, a representative from Calumet County, which borders Lake Winnebago, spoke up in defense of spearing. "I think it is just as easy for the fellows from Shawano and northern and southern counties to come to Lake Winnebago and spear sturgeon as it is for all other counties," he said. "We have the only sturgeon in the state of Wisconsin in quantities large enough to spear. We want our sturgeon spearing through the ice."

Leppla went on to explain that sturgeon spearing is highly dependent on the clarity of the water—it's nearly impossible to spear something you can't see. So while some years many sturgeon might be taken, these times would be balanced by years with terrible, murky water. "You can go out there and sit day after day and possibly not get a sturgeon," he said. Therefore, he believed it should be "all right for good sportsmen who enjoy sturgeon spearing to go out there and sit. If you know anything about sitting on Lake Winnebago when it is anywhere from 10 to 25 below zero—if you are going to go out there and sit, my hat goes off to you."

Leppla seemed to make his point to the rest of the county representatives, as they began to view sturgeon spearing as a recreational activity that was important to the local culture. "There are not many sturgeon speared. It is more or less for sport," said a representative from Manitowoc County. "Let's work with these counties. . . . I don't think we should take their sport away from them."[26] So as the ice fishing debates continued, sturgeon spearing emerged as a unique sport and the preferred, acceptable method for fishermen to hunt a formidable fish. If you wanted to take home a sturgeon, you would have to sit out on a frozen lake and wait for it.

This movable billboard was aimed at passing motorists along State Highway 20 in Illinois in 1938. As tourism became an important part of Wisconsin's economy, many resort owners started questioning whether ice fishing—and spearing—made it more difficult for tourists to catch fish in the summer.

Warden Kramer (right) and an assistant examine two sturgeon taken from a confiscated snag line in 1942.

Despite all of the deliberations at the meeting, many delegates lost sight of the fact that they were only an advisory board; the ultimate decisions would be made by the Conservation Commission. And when the commission released the new fishing laws in December, all hook-and-line fishing was slated to close on January 15, and sturgeon spearing would last only until February 15—shortening the season by a full month.

The announcement did not go over well in Calumet County. In fact, residents there felt as though the wool had been pulled over their eyes. In response, the local sporting clubs banded together and issued a resolution demanding a longer season for both spearing and ice fishing. They sent it to the Conservation Commission and to the governor-elect, Julius P. Heil, who—as the resolution stated—was "known to the common man as 'Julius the Just,' because we feel our stand is just and that we should have a little more justice."[27]

Put on the defensive, Conservation Director H. W. MacKenzie wrote a six-page letter to Heil explaining the situation and why certain decisions had been made. "With respect to the complaints arising from the Lake Winnebago area, I should like to state that for many, many years, the waters of Lake Winnebago and its tributaries have had, by far, more liberal privileges regarding fishing than any other area in the state," he wrote. "It has been a difficult job for the conservation commission to educate people in that area that such continued ruthless taking of fish from those waters was causing a depletion of game fish and sturgeon and that if measures were not taken to protect a basic stock of brood fish, the game fish and sturgeon population would soon be exhausted."[28]

The uproar in Calumet County led to a fourteen hundred-name petition and a public hearing in Fond du Lac where nearly six hundred people crammed into the old armory. The meeting not only was a window into the world of ice fishing—it provided insight to the way Lake Winnebago residents viewed the surrounding natural resources.

After the hearing had been called to order, a Fond du Lac man stood up to say that while tourists had the money to buy or rent motorboats, many locals couldn't afford them. Even if they had a canoe or rowboat, the good fishing was several miles out in the lake. If a storm blew up, it would be a long, dangerous trip back to shore. "Those people who can go out when the weather is fine can take undue risks, and those who have motor boats and high-powered boats can do it, too," said the man.

"Most of us who go out winter fishing have neither. In winter we can take our cars out there, enjoy a day's fishing, and come home."[29]

Another argument in support of ice fishing was that chopping holes through the ice actually benefited the fish population, either by providing more oxygen or relieving pressure. "There's the fisherman standing out on the ice freezing," said Joeseph Mucha of Neenah. "He chops a hole in the ice. What does that hole in the ice do? It takes the pressure off the water so that the fish won't die. It is the pressure of the ice which causes the death of the fish. Take some old tin can, fill it with water, and in the morning your bottom is broken out of it."[30]

As the evening wore on, what it really came down to in the end was who had the right to make decisions about the lake. "We believe in majority rule all the time. If we're in the majority, I don't see why we can't have our winter fishing," said another Fond du Lac man. "When that lake needs to be closed, I believe we could get this many here again to speak in favor of closing it. But, as far as I can see, there isn't a decent argument in favor of closing it at this time."

He continued, "It is our lake; we fish on it, and we know the conditions that exist out there. Our petition shows what the people really want."

This was a revealing statement, because it was completely contrary to the way the Conservation Commission managed the state's natural resources. "The fact is well known that fish and game are the property of the state and the conservation commission acts as custodian of such fish and game," the commission had written to the Calumet County Sportsman's Club a week before the public hearing. "It is not reasonable to assume that the fish and game, whose habitat is in the vicinity of certain towns and villages, are any more the property of the individuals of that vicinity than any other resident of this state. . . . Likewise the commission feels that the fish in Lake Winnebago are the property of the entire state rather than subject to the ownership of the residents of that particular locality."[31]

Suddenly, the crux of the disagreement was clear: people around Lake Winnebago saw the fish as theirs, and the Conservation Commission was trying to regulate it as a resource belonging to the whole state.

Then a question came from the crowd—what did the Conservation Commission base its regulations on, anyway?

Howard Leppla, who had defended spearing at the earlier Conservation Congress meeting in July, stood up and said that he had recently asked Ed

A Foul Smell at the State Capitol

Any new regulatory agency goes through some growing pains, and it was no different for Wisconsin's fledgling conservation department. While wardens had been busy making arrests and confiscating illegally captured fish and game since the 1880s, it wasn't until the 1930s that the Conservation Commission thought to ask what was actually happening with these valuable furs and meat.[1]

It turned out that with no clear system in place, wardens were selling the goods on their own, supposedly sending the proceeds back to Madison to supplement the conservation coffers. When this arrangement was finally discovered by the administrators at the state capitol, suspicions ran rampant. Immediately the rules were ironed out so that confiscated property would be sent directly to Madison to be "disposed of either by currently private sale or at the periodic sales held under the direction of the Chief Warden with the approval of the Director."[2]

The rule was formalized during the summer of 1932. A few months later, something smelled very fishy at the state capitol building.

The Song of the Sturgeon Is Ended, But the Capitol's Melody Lingers On

Wisconsin State Journal, October 19, 1932

Somebody once said, maybe it was Arthur Brisbane or Calvin Coolidge, that an over-ripe fish is very annoying to the human nose.

State employees whose offices are in the east wing of the capitol consider this a gross understatement. They are willing to go on record that there is nothing worse than an over ripe fish and that an over-ripe sturgeon is the worst of all fish.

DEER JOINS FISH

Some time ago a conservation warden seized a sturgeon, which was caught illegally, and deposited it in the vault in the basement of the capitol in the east wing where all articles confiscated by the conservation department are kept. A piece of confiscated venison was also placed in the vault, but the sturgeon constituted the bigger error.

The vault is near the east wing elevator shafts and directly beneath the supreme court chambers. In due time nature took its course and from the sturgeon there began to emanate an odor which was a bit salty.

DIGNIFIED NOSES ASSAILED

As time went on, the odor became saltier, not to say frightful. Whenever the vault door was opened there wafted up through the elevator shaft a smell which was not conducive to work, especially legal work. The supreme court maintained its dignity and made no complaint, although it is understood that some of the justices made sure that the statute giving the court the right to abate a nuisance was still on the books.

The elevator operators were not so dignified. In fact, they were downright irritated. They sprinkled the elevator with moth balls, a move which did a great deal to alleviate the spell of the sturgeon, which by this time was being aided and abetted by the piece of venison, but it wasn't so good for people who don't like moth balls.

One elevator operator was musing bitterly about the situation this morning.

Conservation administrators eventually reverted to the old system of wardens selling confiscated goods on their own. However, they also instituted better documentation, as seen with this 1940 confiscation ticket issued to Haze Diemel Sr. of Leeman.

THE EXPERT GOES TO WORK

"If it had been a private institution, there would have been 96 inspectors here," he remarked.

But in the meantime, Tony Pickarts, a janitor, had been turned loose on the problem. Pickarts won the undying respect and admiration of capitol employees about two years ago when he captured and killed a skunk near the capitol and skinned it there. As a result of this coup, the capitol was practically closed for one day. With unerring instinct, Pickarts located the source of the trouble and removed what was left of the sturgeon and the piece of venison. Then he scrubbed the spot where they had been. But he under-estimated the strength of a dead sturgeon. The odor had seeped into the concrete and had become part of it.

THE MELODY LINGERS ON

Pickarts was stumped. The song was ended, so to speak, but the melody lingered on. Finally, Pickarts went into a huddle with an executive in the capitol.

"Can you tell me some chemical which smells worse than a sturgeon which has been dead for a long time?" he asked.

It was his theory that the way to overcome the odor was to find something that was more odiferous. A discussion followed and it was decided that the remedy might be worse than the disease, so Pickarts was advised to use the ordinary chemicals which are on sale for that purpose. He did so and the spell of the sturgeon is rapidly disappearing from the capital [sic], although the odor of moth balls still clings to the elevator. As for most of the capitol employees, they have repudiated everything connected with a sturgeon, including caviar.

NOTES

1. William Mauthe, chairman, Conservation Commission, to Paul D. Kelleter, conservation director, letter, July 7, 1930, Series 271, Box 19, Folder 3, Wisconsin Historical Society Archives, Madison, WI.

2. Paul D. Kelleter, conservation director, to William Mauthe, chairman, Conservation Commission, letter, April 1, 1931, Series 271, Box 19, Folder 3, Wisconsin Historical Society Archives, Madison, WI.

Michael Goyke (left) and Arthur Hafermen, both commercial fisherman, display a fine catch of sturgeon in 1913, two years before the state moratorium on sturgeon harvest. The large fish on the right was reported to weigh 187½ pounds and measure seventy-nine inches long. All of the fish were caught on set lines in Lake Winnebago near Taycheedah.

Schneberger, the new state fisheries biologist, a few questions about the sturgeon population in Lake Winnebago. Namely, what was the estimated population, how many sturgeon were removed for each of the previous ten years, and what was the estimated increase or decrease in sturgeon during that time. He said that Schneberger hadn't been able to answer any of the questions.

Clearly, more needed to be known about the sturgeon population. So from then on, the Conservation Commission formed an agreement with sturgeon spearers—the spearers would go along with the rules, as long as the commission could provide hard evidence to back those rules up. The agreement would usher in a new era of scientific studies to uncover the secrets of the ancient fish. These studies would lead to regulations that would allow spearers to keep their sport while still keeping the sturgeon population at a healthy level. But it wouldn't be the last time that state managers would hear from discontented sturgeon spearers. Forty years later, the next generation of spearers would take the science of sturgeon into their own hands.

BENEATH THE ICE

This studio portrait from the 1870s is of a spearer with his decoy and catch—a small sturgeon.

Previous page: Spearers drive out to their shanties on frozen Lake Winnebago before sunrise for opening day of the season.

Winters in Wisconsin can be cold and dark. It's lovely weather for the holidays, but by the time the calendar flips to February, a sort of dull, repetitive monotony can set in. As people living around Lake Winnebago pack away the last of their Christmas lights and put another pot of chili on the stove, sturgeon swimming beneath the iced-over lake are engaged in their own winter rituals. Some of them are preparing to move upriver to spawn once the water warms in a few months. Others are just lying low—and for bottom dwellers, that's a natural, easy thing to do.

It's a calm and quiet scene beneath the ice. The roar of outboard motors is gone, and so are the waves from the wind and the water skiers. As the largest creatures milling around in this serene, watery world, sturgeon get to live the high life—no predators, no annoyances, just quiet time spent cruising the lake bottom for red worms and other tasty creatures. Each day is pretty much the same, and while this could drive some people crazy, predictability is a fine thing for a fish.

However, in February, predictability turns into a series of peculiarities. An incessant series of buzzes pierces through the quiet, and suddenly there is light—large rectangles of light peppered all over the ice. Puzzling objects plop down in the water. Some of them are familiar, with a few unique twists. Others are shiny, odd, and utterly foreign. And a few are just so intriguing they demand to be examined up close.

It's sturgeon-spearing season on Lake Winnebago.

Sustenance to Sport

People have been spearing fish ever since they realized it was much easier than trying to grab one with their hands. References to spearing appear in the *Odyssey* and in the Bible, although there is some disagreement about whether or not the spear was the first method of fishing.[1] Native Americans in the Great Lakes region were spearing fish long before Europeans arrived in North America. Some of the earliest French explorers to Wisconsin wrote about their encounters with the Menominee tribe, noting their skill at spearing sturgeon from small canoes in the

midst of churning rapids.[2] Spearing at night seemed to make the most dramatic impression, when flaming torches were used to attract fish to the water's surface.

The Europeans also noted that spearing was a year-round activity. Father Samuel Mazzuchelli was a Dominican missionary who served among the Menominee tribe from 1830 to 1834. In his writings, he noted that the winter fishing season was one of the best times to do mission work, because so many of the tribal members gathered along Green Bay or Lake Winnebago to be near the sturgeon fishing grounds.[3] In 1834, Mazzuchelli described the tribe's method of winter fishing:

> *The Indians . . . make a hole in the ice about a yard across, and let down by a cord a little wooden fish which they keep in motion. Stretched at full length with head over the hole and under cover the better to see below the ice, they watch for the sturgeon as he makes for the little wooden decoy. Then the skillful Indian with a barb fastened to a pole spears the sturgeon, which, after a useless struggle, becomes his prey. This is the principal means by which many Indians get their food in winter.*[4]

Just as they did with many Native American customs and habits, French explorers and traders adopted the ice spearing technique as a tried-and-true way to secure fresh fish during the long winters. However, the Americans who began to settle in the Green Bay area in the 1800s didn't seem to have much interest in peering down holes in the ice. Many of them were willing to spear sturgeon in

A wooden sturgeon decoy carved by Tom Tittl in 1997.

Early French explorers and traders learned to spear fish through the ice from the tribes living in the Great Lakes region. Covering one's head with a blanket eventually evolved into constructing a "dark-house" or ice shanty.

the spring, when plucking a spawning sturgeon out of the Wolf River was as easy as picking an apple out of a tree. But it appears that winter spearing for sturgeon didn't pick up in earnest until the 1870s when a series of economic recessions and high unemployment sent people out onto the ice looking for extra income and food for the table. Throughout a twenty-year period, local newspapers describe more than one hundred men out on the ice during the winters. "Many of them who are engaged in it do so to support their families while others do it for the sport there is in it," was the report from Oshkosh in January 1895.[5]

Nearly ten years earlier, J. O. Roorbach wrote about a winter he had spent in Green Bay in the 1850s and the "curious Indian custom" of spearing through the ice. He persuaded one spearer to teach him the method, and he was impressed by the range of motion of the decoy:

> . . . *the wooden decoy-fish, meanwhile, was being delicately handled by the Indian fisherman, now raised gently to the top of the water, then sinking slowly. The very action of sinking and the position of its artificial fins made it run forward, now this way, now that, until it really seemed alive.*[6]

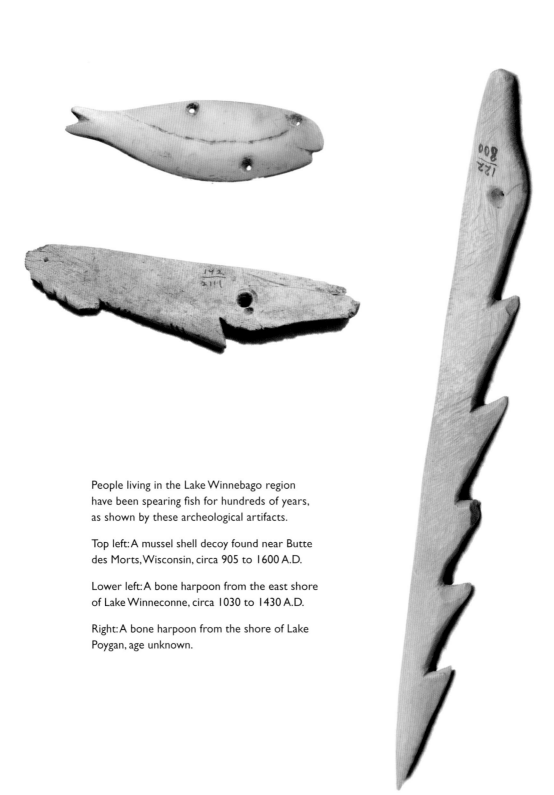

People living in the Lake Winnebago region have been spearing fish for hundreds of years, as shown by these archeological artifacts.

Top left: A mussel shell decoy found near Butte des Morts, Wisconsin, circa 905 to 1600 A.D.

Lower left: A bone harpoon from the east shore of Lake Winneconne, circa 1030 to 1430 A.D.

Right: A bone harpoon from the shore of Lake Poygan, age unknown.

If you're lucky enough to see one, a sturgeon looks like a large, torpedo-shaped shadow drifting by. This photo is one of the few taken of a sturgeon swimming past the hole in a shanty, thanks to very clear water and a very lucky photographer. The white coffee cup in the bottom left corner shows the spearer's decoy choice for the day.

When the water in Lake Winnebago is murky, spearers often lower two white PVC pipes to the bottom of the lake. The pipes are tied together to form an "X" that provides a bright background to better see a sturgeon. In the past, people threw all sorts of bright things down into the hole to help improve sturgeon sighting: eggshells, sliced potatoes, navy beans, white lime, sheets of pulp from the paper mills, corn, noodles, and paper plates. It made the bottom of Lake Winnebago a messy place, so today anything you put in the hole has to come back out.

Like many other curious observers of spearing fish through the ice, Roorbach decided to try it himself several years later, with one noticeable—and comfortable— adaptation. Apparently he was not the sort to tuck himself up in a makeshift tepee or lie down on a frozen lake, a blanket over his head and his back end exposed to the elements. Instead, his first task was to nail together boards to build a twelve-square-foot shelter, "a grand improvement upon the Indian blanket, making it possible for the sport to be comfortable, as well as exciting and interesting." One of his fishing buddies outdid him by building a thirty-six-square-foot structure with a floor, seat, and a small charcoal stove so that he could "enjoy a change of position, his pipe, or book, at leisure," whenever the fish were absent.[7] Many would say that with the advent of the "darkhouse" or ice shanty, the age of ice fishing for sport officially began.

By the early 1900s, unregulated fishing for sturgeon—by spear, net, and setlines—had taken its toll on the population, and harvesting the fish in any manner was outlawed statewide in 1915. However, as the Great Depression took hold of the nation, sportsmen in Wisconsin began lobbying to regain access to the giant fish. The legislature listened, and in June 1931 the law passed to reopen sturgeon spearing on Lake Winnebago. And although specific rules and regulations have changed over the years, the spearing season has remained open ever since.

In the early days, spearers numbered in the hundreds, if that. "If you were fishing years ago, farmers were the only ones that sturgeon fished," said Vic Schneider, patriarch of a large sturgeon-spearing family based in Taycheedah. "Now everybody sturgeon fishes, the way it seems. They come from far and wide." DNR records confirm Schneider's observations. Four-wheel drive, chainsaws, and comfortable shanties have made it much easier for more people to get out on the ice—today close to ten thousand licenses are sold each year.

Opposite page: Ben Burg of Stockbridge and his friend Dave Hemauer of Colorado decided to build a gigantic shanty so that their families could comfortably come along sturgeon spearing. Affectionately named the "Blue Ox," the shanty had a fireplace, gas stove, bar, bay window, wallpaper on the walls, paneling, and shag carpeting. "We had some good times in that shanty," Burg said. "We almost got a sturgeon in it once." Here Vicky Burg, Jim Burg, Brad Burg, and Jack Patenaude warm themselves by the stove.

Shooting through a Chimney

If you have never had the opportunity to sit in a dark shed on a frozen lake and stare at a hole in the ice, sturgeon spearing may not seem like much of a sport. In fact, with most shanties comfortably heated and insulated, as well as stocked with snacks and Bloody Mary mix, the whole setup may even seem like a well-thought-out escape from one's family during monotonous winter days (to be fair, a 2001 survey found this to be true for only one-fifth of the interviewed sturgeon spearers).[8]

But committing to sit at a hole and wait—days, weeks, years—for a giant fish to meander by, all the while prepared to hurdle a seven-foot hunk of steel through the water, hit the fish as it swims by, and then wrestle it out of the water, is about as sporting as modern-day hunting gets. While many spearers are also avid deer hunters, most will tell you that sturgeon spearing is an entirely different experience. "It's just such a thrill, and it's a one-moment opportunity," said Carl Jersild of Neenah, who has speared just one sturgeon in nineteen years. "It's not like you can sit in a stand and watch something come up to you and then wait your turn. This is just an instantaneous opportunity, and you really have to be 100 percent alert all the time." Many people will tell you that the tedious nature of sturgeon spearing is just like trying to shoot a duck while looking up through a chimney.

However, it's not just the thrill of the hunt that pulls spearers out on the ice every year, trailing their shanties behind them. Sturgeon spearing is a ritual, one that many people have performed their whole lives, passed down from their parents, grandparents, and great-grandparents. And in the dead of winter, it's a terrific excuse to get outside and see what the neighbors are up to. Dan Gerhardt, like many other spearers, prefers to sit by himself, but he'll also say that what he enjoys most about sturgeon spearing is the camaraderie. After six hours of solitude in his shanty, he looks forward to meeting up with friends to compare stories. For some spearers, the logical place to congregate is at one of the local taverns scattered around the lake, many of which also double as sturgeon-registration stations run by the DNR. But some people prefer to stay on the ice, setting up chairs and grills outside their shanty in classic tailgate fashion. As LeRoy Remme from Appleton said, "Some people go to church to see everybody, and at sturgeon time, they go out on Lake Winnebago to see everybody."

Above: Don and Ron Mathies, brothers from Minnesota, enjoy lunch at Trip's Bar and Grill in Pipe, Wisconsin, on opening day of sturgeon spearing. Five years ago they gave spearing a try, and they've been making the seven-hour drive to Lake Winnebago every year since.

If you walk around and visit some of the shanties or stop by a tavern later in the afternoon, it's easy to find out how people first became hooked on sturgeon spearing. Dan Gerhardt (left) was born in Neenah in 1940 and has been fishing on Lake Winnebago most of his life. When he was a young boy, his father took him out to his ice shanty. His dad's friends were out on the ice, too, and he remembers making the rounds to see all of them. "I'd go around and visit with these guys, and I was just fascinated by the smell of the inside of the shanty," he said. A distinct odor wafted from the primitive woodstoves, but there was another scent much more interesting to an eight-year-old boy. "If somebody did get a fish, you could smell the fish slime on the floor," said Gerhardt. "I was just mesmerized by it."

Cutting holes and hauling shanties out on the ice used to be hard work and kept the numbers of sturgeon spearers low. Today, plows, bridges, chainsaws, and comfortable shanties have caused a surge in the popularity of the sport.

Left: Nancy Schneider and Douglas Gregoire embrace after "blessing" a newly cut sturgeon hole with brandy.

Simply setting up to go sturgeon spearing is a ritual in itself. First, a hole needs to be cut through the ice. In the past, using only hand tools, the difficulty of this task depended on the thickness of the ice and how many friends could be convinced to help. Two holes were chiseled out, just big enough to fit the width of an ice saw, and a square or rectangle was sawed by hand. The resulting ice slab was pushed under the ice with pike poles. Clement Van Gompel from Kimberly used to cut holes with Joe Wilz, his boss at a local canning plant. Van Gompel recalled that even though he and Wilz labored in subzero temperatures, they always worked up a sweat cutting holes, especially during those winters when up to three feet of ice covered the lakes. It would take a couple of days to tow shanties out on the ice, cut holes, and get everything ready for opening day.

Nowadays, chainsaws have speeded things up. Cutting a hole can take as little as ten minutes, and the sides of the hole can be angled outward, improving visibility so that a sturgeon can be spotted before it actually enters the area of the hole. This isn't a big deal when the ice is fairly thin, but when you're cutting through two feet or more, an angled edge increases the field of vision considerably and could be the difference between a missed throw and a trophy fish.

It may seem too obvious to state, but ice is always the most critical component of ice fishing. It affects where you can set up, how long it takes to cut a hole, and your mode of transportation. The official word is that ice is never 100 percent safe, because its thickness can vary dramatically from place to place on the lake, and cracks and shoves change almost daily. However, the general rule of thumb is that a foot or more is needed to drive right out onto the lake with a car or truck. If the ice is less than a foot thick, a snowmobile or all-terrain vehicle is the only safe bet, and less than three inches—well, you shouldn't even be walking on it. Every winter at least one vehicle breaks through the ice and plunges into the water. It used to be that people would just drive old beaters out onto the ice and take their chances, abandoning the cars if they ever succumbed to the depths of Lake Winnebago. But times have changed. Owners of sunken vehicles are responsible by law for reclaiming them from the lake. In fact, there is a tidy business done during the winter from towing vehicles out of the lake. A deep-water diving job with a lot of ice to cut through might run around three thousand dollars if you call the appropriately named business, SUNK.

It's not just the thickness of ice that matters. As solid as it appears, ice is still a fluid substance that shifts and moves with changes in temperature and wind.

Shacks are used by ice fishermen angling for all sorts of fish, but what makes a spearing shanty unique is that it lacks windows, or the windows are covered up. This is why spearing shanties are also called "darkhouses." Complete darkness is needed so that only the hole is illuminated and—if the water is clear—a sturgeon can be easily spotted.

The key to spearing a sturgeon is patience. Many spearers describe staring into the incandescent hole as being just like staring at a blank TV screen. The only light within a sturgeon shanty comes from the hole—an eerie, green hue of sunlight filtered through the snow and ice on the frozen lake.

Above left: Leo A. Schoebel was an Allis-Chalmers tractor dealer in Fond du Lac. Here he displays both a new tractor and a 142-pound, 80-inch sturgeon he speared in February 1946 at Lakeside Park. His great-grandson Luke Ladwig hangs this photo in his shanty every winter for good luck.

Above right: Bill Buksyk, of Neenah, wanted to go spearing one winter, but he didn't want to leave his pregnant wife at home alone. He solved the predicament by bringing her along. That year the ice shifted tremendously, creating a huge wall blocking their route off the lake. Luckily, a friend was nearby to direct them home. "I was afraid it was gonna be baby time right on Lake Winnebago," Buksyk said. He admits that was the one time he was scared on the lake, but he didn't tell his wife.

Large cracks appear, or ice piles up, walling off a main driving route back to shore. Sometimes the movement is hardly noticeable. One year, Carl Jersild was using a decoy marker in the center of the hole that was fixed to the lake bottom with a weight. He was sitting with a friend, watching the hole, when they noticed that the marker was at the edge of the hole. Jersild picked it up and recentered it in the hole, but within a half hour it was back at the edge again. He and his buddy didn't think much of it until they left the lake that day and saw a huge pile up of ice on the shore. That's when they realized that it wasn't the decoy marker that had moved—it was the ice under the shanty. "It must have moved about six or eight feet, and we were on that ice while it was moving and didn't even know it," Jersild said.

Once the ice is at least a foot thick, a sort of highway system is established on the lake to help residents of the temporary shantytown get around. For the past forty years or more, local fishing clubs have plowed and maintained roads for winter ice fishing and sturgeon spearing. They mark the highway system with leftover evergreen Christmas trees and place bridges over major cracks in the ice.

One of the largest fish speared on opening day is displayed at a party in Vic Schneider's workshop near Fond du Lac. The fish was a 135-pound female measuring seventy-two inches; it was speared by Denis "Buzz" Henen of Appleton.

SURFACING SUBMARINE

LeRoy Remme had been sturgeon spearing for only three years when he landed one of the largest fish ever recorded on Lake Winnebago in 1990. Remme and his wife Kay had been sitting in the shanty for twenty minutes when they caught the first glimpse of the sturgeon.

All I saw was the backside of him, the tail part, but it was huge. I thought, "Oh boy, I just missed my chance." I did throw the spear, anyhow, just for practice, I guess. Brought it back up, got it all set again, and about fifteen or twenty minutes later, here he comes back again.

The fish came right up to the decoy in sixteen feet of water. Remme remembered that the water was so clear that year, you could see a dime on the lake bottom— "gin clear," as many describe it. He threw the spear again, successfully this time, and then he and his wife wrangled the sturgeon up into the hole. The fish was 144 pounds, seventy-four inches long, with a girth of thirty-eight inches. Remme said it sounded like a submarine surfacing when it finally popped out of the water.

As we got the fish up into the hole, it was so heavy it took like three times for me to get him out of the shanty and out of the door. Both of us went. As I hit the ice, I'm laying alongside the fish, and here come a guy with a station wagon. He thought I speared myself. He got out of his station wagon and didn't take his car out of gear. It kept going and bumped up against another guy's shanty.

The sturgeon was the largest speared that year. Remme mounted the trophy fish and took it on tour to a few local establishments. It's too large to hang anywhere in his house, so it now resides in his son Mike's taxidermy shop in Fremont.

David Bretthauer (right) speared his first sturgeon off of Waverly Beach in February 1935. It was a double (perhaps triple) blessing, as his wife, Rose (left), was expecting twin girls in a few months. The Bretthauers, both deaf, excitedly told all their friends and family about the sturgeon. "Can you imagine all the hands flying around telling this great story?" daughters Mary Ann Miller and Rose Kofnetka later said.

Spearers from earlier days had no such luxuries, and many people didn't mark their own fishing holes—much to the surprise of people who discovered them by falling in. With so few people out on the ice, everyone had to watch out for themselves. In case of a sudden snowstorm, it was always wise to take a compass along to help direct you off the ice and a shovel to dig out your vehicle—or horse.

Sometimes horses could be the more reliable transportation. Willard Jenkins of Pipe remembers one year on the frozen lake when his horse stopped walking and wouldn't go forward. "So we walked ahead of the horse, and all at once—boom. We went right down through it," he said. Apparently there was a significant crack that was covered by barely an inch of ice, "and that horse knew that," Jenkins said. "Now how the hell he knew that, I don't know."

Even though some aspects of sturgeon spearing have changed over the years, one thing remains the same: when a spear actually makes contact with a good-sized sturgeon, all hell breaks loose. The trick is to keep the sturgeon from doing the same. Any fish can put up a good fight, but a six-foot, 175-pound sturgeon can easily win.

The actual process of spearing a sturgeon and then pulling it out of the hole, through the door of the shanty, and out onto the ice is often a blur for many spearers. "It's pure adrenaline, that's what it is," said Mike Remme of Fremont. "From the time you see that fish, to getting it out the door, a lot of times you don't even remember what all happened." But it's that primal rush of adrenaline that keeps people returning to the ice every year—or, in the case of ninety-year-old Donald Peterson Sr., wishing he could. "I dream about it," he said. "I wish I could be out there, you know. And, it hurts."

Mary Boettcher, with her parents Vic and Mary Lou Schneider, hugs the first sturgeon she ever speared.

June Burg and her fellow women spearers: (seated) Polly Krueger, Tina Burg, Rupert the Dog, Jeanie Schmid, Natalie Krueger, Alexis Schwobe, and Theresa Stumpf (standing) Jennifer Westenberger, Kelly Krueger, Wendy Schwobe, Jane Dedering, Melissa Burg, Dorothy Levknecht, and June Burg.

CALL THEM "FISHERWOMEN"

For a long time, whenever a woman appeared at a registration station with a speared sturgeon, she drew suspicion.

The rumor around Lake Winnebago was that a man would spear a sturgeon and then ask his wife to go register it in her own name. The man, meanwhile, would return to his shanty in hopes of spearing yet another fish.

It was an easy way to sidestep the law of one-sturgeon-per-person, but it was illegal nonetheless. And in the early 1990s, wardens decided to put an end to it.

According to some women, wardens were especially nosey that year, asking question after question about how the sturgeon was speared, how deep in the water it was, where on the lake was it taken from, and what time of day was it speared. A local newspaper editor defended the cross-examinations. "Of all the sturgeon licenses purchased, only about 7 or 8 percent are purchased by women. Of the licenses purchased by women, about 50 percent are filled. The success ratio for men is between 20 and 30 percent. Does anyone really expect game wardens to believe that women are twice as good at spearing sturgeon as men?"[1]

June Burg of Stockbridge grew up sturgeon fishing with her father, and she was furious when she read the editorial. She wrote back, "Do you think we put on all these clothes everyday and pack all these bologna sandwiches just on the pretense that we might get to tag someone else's fish? What a thrill!"

Mary Lou Schneider speared this 107-pound sturgeon in 1967.

On your ratio figures, maybe women are better spearers than men, or maybe it's because the women are doing the fishing while their husbands are out socializing," she continued. "My mother fishes, my sisters fish, my daughters fish, my daughter-in-law fishes . . . don't say that a woman with a sturgeon is suspicious. Most women with a sturgeon are 'fisherwomen.'"

Irene Halfman in 1952 (left) and in 1979 (right).

NOTE

1. Tom Woodrow, "Wardens Harassing Women?" *Appleton Post Crescent*, February 24, 1990 (from June Burg's scrapbook).

Irene Halfmann (above, with her husband, Greg) of Malone, Wisconsin, speared a ninety-two pound sturgeon in 1979. She remembers saying to herself, "Good Lord, not so big!" when she saw it, because she was all alone in the shanty. She wrapped the fish in a rug and hoisted it up into her truck by herself.

Lynn Benedict of Winneconne, Wisconsin, started spearing when she married her husband, Larry, 52 years ago. She was alone when she speared her first sturgeon, in 1958, (left) and this became her preferred way of fishing. She has speared quite a few fish while alone, the largest weighing 102 pounds.

Sue Hopp of Berlin, Wisconsin, remembers when a warden knocked on her shanty one blustery day and was surprised to find her alone. "Can't a woman spear by herself?" she replied. Here she is with her husband, Clarence.

FISHING FOR HARD TIMES

When Black Tuesday hit Wall Street in 1929, Reuben Hoelzel was a thirteen-year-old boy living on his family's farm on the east side of Lake Winnebago near Stockbridge. As the Depression wore on for the next decade, prices for grain, milk, and hogs fell dramatically.

The eldest of seven children, Hoelzel stopped attending school at the sixth grade in order to help on the eighty-acre farm. Ice fishing for walleyes and pike helped feed the family during the winter. And when he was sixteen, he started to spear sturgeon using two-by-six boards for runners and a team of horses, to pull his shanty out on the ice.

"There was a lot of snow in those earlier years, and the roads were mostly shut," Hoelzel recalled. "We'd have to go through the field down on our farm, cut the fence, cut the fence on the next farm . . . go down on the next road, and go down 'til we got to Highway 55 and then to Stockbridge, and then out . . . to the lake." Apparently fixing fences was a common chore in the spring.

Hoelzel made his own decoys from scrap wood, fashioning fins out of metal and adding lead to weigh them down. The lead and fins had to be placed precisely in order for the decoy to move realistically in the water. He made his spears out of pitchforks by welding barbs on the sides of the tines and adding a heavy pipe to give it weight. Most of the sturgeon he speared were forty to fifty pounds.

Hoelzel remembered that days he brought sturgeon home resulted in a big feast. His mother would fry them up for breakfast along with fried potatoes—a satisfying meal after a long morning of chores. While farm families probably ate better than many out-of-work city people during the Depression, Hoelzel knew that his family just scraped by and was very lucky not to lose the farm. "We ate a lot of lard, too!" he said.

Opposite page: Four generations of Hoelzels: Reuben, age ninety-two, Wayne, sixty-one, Brian, thirty-eight, and Carter, three

Clem Van Gompel speared this 76-inch-long sturgeon in 1972. He let his father pull it up out of the hole. "That was my dad's first and only experience with a sturgeon, and his knees were shaking when he finished," Van Gompel said.

THE FIRST THROW

Jerry Neumueller grew up in Oshkosh and worked as a bricklayer in the early 1960s. On one job site, he met a mason named Mel Burholtz who couldn't stop talking about sturgeon whenever the spearing season drew near. Neumueller grew curious and finally asked Burholtz if he could accompany him out on the ice to see for himself what all the fuss was about.

They had been sitting in the shanty for a few hours on opening day, when Burholtz decided to "make the rounds" to see his friends, leaving Neumueller alone to stare down into the sixteen-foot-deep water.

"I remember he wasn't out the door more than ten seconds," Neumueller recalled. "I saw a sturgeon coming in . . . out in front of me, coming in on the left side. I could see it right along bottom 'cause it was so clear. . . . I remember yellin' out, and I says, 'Now here comes one. What do I do?' And he says, well, he says, 'You take the spear and you throw at it.' And not knowing the situation and pretty excited about it and stuff like that, I just picked up the spear and I threw the spear at the fish as it was coming in, which I knew afterwards was a total mistake—I should have waited 'til it came right in underneath me and then threw. But I threw out ahead of me and the spear went off to the side and it went over the fish because the fish was coming towards me."

Neumueller learned from his first experience, and at least thirty years went by before he ever missed again. He speared over a dozen sturgeon in his lifetime, and although he always enjoyed eating them—whether smoked, baked, or fried—he also relished the chance to view a different world.

"I spent a lot of time on a boat, on top of the water, and this was a chance to see what's going around swimming in the water." He said that when the water was clear, you could see all sorts of creatures that you could only imagine were swimming below your boat. "The sensation you get of looking into that type of water, it's just a different feeling and it just keeps you interested, keeps you going, and keeps bringing you back that way."

BEGINNER'S LUCK

Gwen Bowe had spent time with friends in their shanties, and in 1980 she decided to try spearing for herself. Her husband Ken helped her get everything set up. After he left, Bowe realized just what sturgeon spearing is all about—sitting alone looking at a hole in the ice for hours.

When the day was nearly over, she pulled the decoy out of the water and stepped outside to see if her husband was coming to pick her up. No sign of him. She went back inside to wait when she saw a dark mass moving through the hole and thought, "This has to be a sturgeon."

She didn't even get to throw the spear (it was more like a jab), because the fish was only three feet from the surface—and it looked huge.

"After I speared it, then it took off and dived towards the bottom," she remembered. The fish writhed around with the spearhead lodged in its back, but Bowe managed to pull it to the surface, secure it with a gaff hook, and burst through the shanty door.

The sturgeon turned out to be 126 pounds, seventy-four inches long, with a girth of thirty-two inches—a record fish for that season that earned her a trophy.

Bowe had the fish mounted and installed in a case at a local supper club, but it now resides on display at Pace University in New York. It was requested by a professor of environmental law, Robert F. Kennedy Jr., and hand-delivered by Bill and Kathy Casper of Oshkosh. Kennedy had a plaque made in Bowe's honor, and she's happy that many people can see her sturgeon.

Elroy Schroeder of Appleton speared this 180-pound sturgeon (top) in 1953. It held the record as the largest sturgeon speared on Lake Winnebago until 2004, when Dave Piechowski of Redgranite brought in a 188-pound sturgeon (bottom).

THE ONE THAT GOT AWAY

Although many aspects of sturgeon spearing have become easier and more comfortable over the years, Lake Winnebago can still be a dangerous place. Harry Kachur, who lives on the north shore of the lake near Waverly Beach, sums up his thirty years of spearing like this: "I've not had a lot of luck on the ice is what it amounts to."

Kachur isn't referring to the twenty-two years he spent out on the ice before he speared his first sturgeon. No, he's talking about a series of mishaps that range from comical to nearly catastrophic. Once, when sitting in a shanty with a friend, Kachur went to light the stove without realizing that his buddy had already turned on the gas. Boom!—the stove blew up. Another time, a friend's truck broke through the ice, and while Kachur was trying to help rescue it, he slipped and broke his leg.

However, these incidents pale in comparison to the legendary story that's told and retold all around Lake Winnebago.

In 2000, Kachur and his friend Bruce Nickles drove out on the ice off of Fresh Air Camp near Neenah. Nickles dropped Kachur off at his shanty and then headed to his own, a little distance away. It was a windy morning, and the snow had just started to fall. Inside the shanty, Kachur was setting things up and getting settled when he suddenly got a kink in his knee, lost his balance, and fell in the ice hole.

As he plunged into the frigid water, Kachur knocked his spear off the hook. The heavy spear followed him into the hole and pierced the side of his face. While still underwater, Kachur grabbed hold of the spearhead and yanked it out, which severely cut his face and ear, but allowed him to finally make it back to the water's surface.

A three-hundred-pound man, Kachur now struggled to pull himself out of the hole, which was eight inches below the floor of the shanty. He was weighed down with big sub-zero boots and heavy, insulated clothes that soaked up the icy water and pulled him down like a block of concrete. Unable to get out, he yelled for Nickles out the shanty door that was now ajar, but the howling wind was blowing in the wrong direction for his friend to hear his calls.

Lake Winnebago had its hold on Kachur. Weak from the cold and blood loss, and knowing his chances of being rescued were slim, he turned his thoughts to practical matters.

"I had that presence of mind . . . I was thinking, 'I'm just gonna tie this rope around me, this spear rope, so at least they won't have to look for me, you know. I won't come floating up in the spring.'"

Meanwhile, Nickles had taken a look outside and saw that the door of Kachur's shanty was ajar. He drove over and found his friend barely coherent with a rope tied around his waist. Nickles quickly grabbed Kachur by the belt and in one mighty effort pulled him out of the water. Then he ran outside for help.

Bob Frank and his brother Red were out on the ice that morning, too. They had decided to have another cup of coffee and wait the storm out. An hour later they emerged from their shanty and saw a man a ways off waving both arms in the air.

"That isn't right," Bob said. "We better go over there."

Bob and Red drove over and followed Bruce into the shanty, where Kachur lay blue and unable to speak. With Red taking his legs and an arm apiece for Bob and Bruce, they heaved Kachur up onto the tailgate of Bruce's truck, just as they would have done with any sturgeon they speared.

By the time they reached the hospital, Kachur's core body temperature was just eighty-eight degrees after spending more than an hour in the water.

Bob figured a few more minutes in the hole, and Kachur wouldn't have survived. He thinks it was luck that he and his brother decided to have that extra cup of coffee.

As for Kachur, he still refers to himself as the three hundred–pounder he speared that got away.

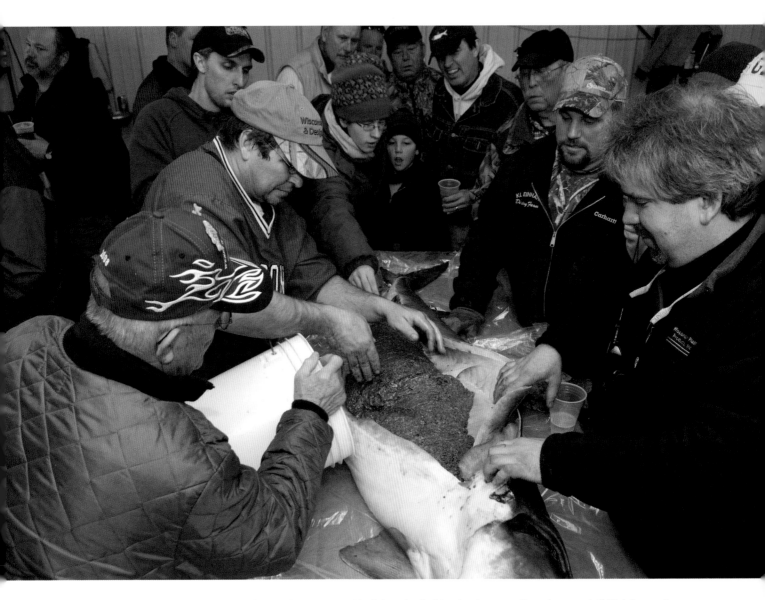

Mike Laack slits the belly of a 150-pound sturgeon, as Vic Schneider holds a bucket to collect the eggs. Jeff Kleinhans of Kiel speared the sturgeon earlier in the day, and Schneider will turn the roe into caviar the next morning.

Cooking up the Catch

Love it or hate it—that's how it goes with eating sturgeon meat. Some people feast on it all winter long, while others just can't get past the fact that it came from such an odd-looking fish. Bill Buksyk thinks the people who don't like the taste probably didn't clean the fish correctly. He advises doing a careful job of cutting out all of the yellow fat, because that's the source of the bad taste. And even though most spearers dream of taking home a hundred-pound fish, the monstrous ones generally don't taste as good as the thirty- to fifty-pounders, according to Clement Van Gompel of Kimberly.

The most common ways to prepare sturgeon are smoking, frying, and baking. Smoking has long been the easiest way to preserve fish, and many people still prefer this method over all others. The result is rich, oily, substantive meat that melts in your mouth like butter. To eat sturgeon fresh, many people cut it up into one-inch steaks, soak it in milk overnight to remove any "fishiness," and then roll it in egg and cracker crumbs and either fry it up or bake it at a low temperature.

And then there's the caviar.

Those spearers who happen to haul in a ripe female sturgeon stumble out of their shanties and into an elite culinary world of briny baby fish. A large female lake sturgeon might be carrying up to sixty pounds of eggs. Sifted and salted, those eggs become caviar, one of the world's most sought-after delicacies. Farmed California white sturgeon produce roe that sells for around one hundred dollars an ounce, and caviar from some sturgeon in the Caspian Sea can cost nearly a thousand dollars an ounce.

But these prices have no value in Wisconsin. State law prohibits the sale of lake sturgeon or its roe.

The law is in place to preserve the lake sturgeon population as well as the sport fishery. The fish are meant to be enjoyed by the public, not by those dining in elite restaurants. Despite being unprofitable, the eggs are not wasted. New York chefs might be aghast to know that caviar is enjoyed freely by many Wisconsinites with a little cream cheese on a saltine cracker, washed down with an ice-cold Miller from the tap.

Richard Braasch has had his hands in just about every aspect of sturgeon spearing—he learned the sport from his father when he was nine; built more than forty shanties for friends and fund-raisers; made his own decoys, spears, and sled saws; and is now president of the West Central Chapter of Sturgeon For Tomorrow. In addition, every spearing season he has his hands—sometimes arms—in buckets full of sturgeon eggs. People who spear a gravid female sturgeon bring the buckets to Braasch's basement, where he transforms the gooey globs into caviar.

It's a lengthy process that involves sifting the eggs through several different handmade screens with various sizes of mesh. After rinsing and straining the roe, Braasch mixes in a precise amount of salt in proportion to the weight of the eggs. The salt preserves the eggs and lengthens their shelf life, but caviar is best enjoyed sooner rather than later. Patricia Braasch helps her husband out by spooning the finished product into small jam jars. They usually return half of the caviar to the spearer, and the rest they give away to friends. "It doesn't take long, and all of a sudden they're gone," Braasch said.

A FAMILY AFFAIR

In 1962, Fritz and Cynthia Wendt bought a tavern overlooking the water on the west side of Lake Winnebago. Ever since, Wendt's on the Lake has been a family-owned business and a hub of sturgeon spearing activity. Fritz helped found the Southwest Chapter of Sturgeon For Tomorrow and served as its first president. His grandson Shawn now serves as secretary.

In addition to providing spearers with a good meal, cold beer, and an inviting atmosphere to share their stories, Wendt's rents shanties to people who don't own their own. In the wee hours of the morning during spearing season, Shawn and his father Mike head out onto the ice to fire up heaters and skim ice off the holes in more than a dozen shanties that are often rented by people from outside the state. "All they have to do is put their decoys down and they're ready to spear," Shawn said.

The Wendts are all spearers themselves, so they can understand the excitement that customers bring into the tavern after a successful day out on the ice. In the early days, before Wendt's was a restaurant, people used to bring their sturgeon right into the bar.

"They would bring them right in here and flop them on the floor with all their excitement and start telling their stories," said Linda Wendt, current owner of Wendt's on the Lake. Her daughter, Anne Marie (Wendt) Ziemer, sometimes finds it difficult to squeeze in sturgeon spearing between working at Wendt's and raising her three children, but when she makes the effort it usually pays off, even if she comes home empty-handed. "One day I went and I sat for three hours and it was the best three hours I've had in three years. It was quiet and relaxing," she said.

Depending on the length of the sturgeon season, the month of February is often the best for business. Altogether, the season produces an annual economic impact of more than three million dollars to the Lake Winnebago region. It's not just the spearers who bring in good business to Wendt's. Plenty of people stop by just to take a look at the giant, frozen fish hauled off the ice. Cynthia and Fritz used to take a photo of anyone who hung their sturgeon on a pole outside the tavern. Today, the photos fill two albums that their great-grandchildren may flip through as part of their family history.

Above: Mike Wendt, Anne Marie (Wendt) Ziemer, Shawn Wendt, and Linda Wendt

Opposite page: Cynthia Wendt

Spearing by the Rules

Sturgeon spearing is strictly regulated, and the rules are regularly tweaked by the DNR and the Winnebago Citizen Sturgeon Advisory Committee. The season can last up to sixteen days in February, but it will end early if any of the preset limits for juvenile females, adult females, or males are reached. Depending on how clear the water happens to be and how easy it is to spot a sturgeon, the season has been as short as two days. That said, sturgeon spearers never oversleep on opening day.

Other Spearing Regulations

BAG LIMIT: one lake sturgeon per license

MINIMUM LENGTH: thirty-six inches

SPEARING HOURS: 6:30 a.m. to 12:30 p.m. No artificial lights of any kind can be used while spearing.

POSSESSION AND USE OF A SPEAR: Spears can be used on the Winnebago lakes only during sturgeon season, and sturgeon can be harvested only with a spear thrown by hand from inside a fishing shelter placed on the ice during spearing season. Angling equipment is not allowed inside a sturgeon-spearing shanty.

ICE HOLE RESTRICTIONS: Ice holes larger than twelve inches in diameter can be used only for spearing sturgeon, and holes may be cut no earlier than forty-eight hours before the spearing season opens. The total area of a sturgeon-spearing hole must not exceed forty-eight square feet. Holes must be marked with at least two strips of wood that extend at least three feet above the ice.

TAGGING REQUIREMENTS: Spearers must attach a valid tag to the sturgeon as soon as it is speared and then register it at a DNR station the same day by 1:30 p.m. While transporting the sturgeon to the registration station, the sturgeon must be in plain view—visible to a person in a passing vehicle.

ICE SHANTIES: All shanties must bear the name and address of the owner, and the door of any occupied shanty must be able to be readily opened from the outside.

A frozen sturgeon waits in line to be registered.

A boy dressed in knickers clears the ice in preparation for fishing next to his family's ice shanty in 1898.

Historically, many people referred to ice spearfishing as the "poor man's sport" because all the necessary gear was—and, for the most part, still is today—made by hand, often out of salvaged materials.[1] Tar paper became walls for an ice shanty, an old pitchfork turned into a spear, and a scrap piece of wood transformed into a fish decoy. Although these tools of the trade all need to fulfill certain basic, utilitarian needs where form definitely follows function, they also provide a canvas to express individual tastes and creativity.

The Ice Shanty

Once holes are cut out of the ice, spearers set up their home away from home. The shanty is positioned over the hole, and snow is packed around the base to block the wind and any stray rays of light. Spearers drill holes into the ice at the corners, drop ropes in, and cover the holes with snow. The ropes, which are tied to the corners of the shanty, freeze into the ice and secure the structure in place.

Over the years, the materials, size, and design of ice shacks have changed as spearers experimented with the ideal shelter for their sport. Sometimes round sawdust bins were used, and they were simply rolled out onto the ice. Others were capped with a cupola to provide enough room to wield a ten-foot-long spear handle but still keep the ceiling low enough to make the shanty as snug and warm as possible.

Staying warm in early shanties was a challenge, as most of them weren't insulated. Jerry Neumueller recalled using small stoves fueled with wood and coal. During the first hour in the morning as the fire was started and the shanty warmed up, moisture would drip from the ceiling, and at night the spearers would cough from the smoke of the coal burning. Soot clouded the water in the hole.

Most of today's shacks are heated by gas stoves complete with thermostats, creating a climate warm enough to remove your hat, gloves, and jacket. Stock the shanty with the basics—chairs, coffeepot, and a little bacon to fry up—or luxuries such as a generator, radio, and satellite television, and you're more than ready for opening day.

Harry Lopas, third from right,
used his 1947 Diamond T Truck
to pull his shanty and four others
out onto Lake Winnebago.
His shanty, on the bed of the
truck, was double-ended, allowing
each of the two spearers to
have his own hole, but still talk
to each other.

Shanties range from luxurious and artistic to thrifty and practical. The oldest shanty displayed here was built by Hobie Gilgenbach of Fond du Lac out of an old steel sawdust bin in the 1940s (top row, center). "If he would get something for nothing and fix it up, he was a happy guy," Gilgenbach's son Lee said.

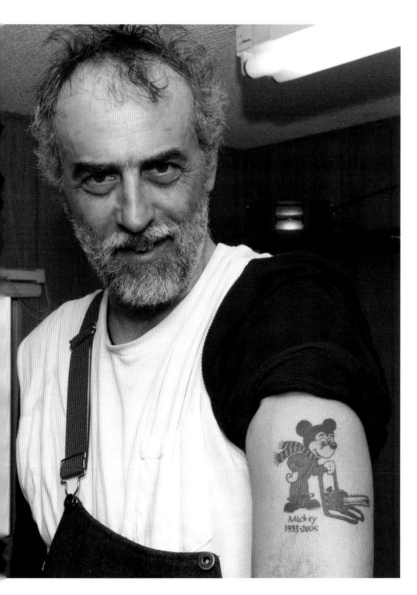

Left: Rowland "Mickey" Keck and "Grandpa Bud" started the Boys' and Girls' Brigade about thirty years ago as a fund-raiser for local youth programs. They built a special chainsaw mounted on a sled to cut sturgeon holes for spearers. Keck died in 2005, and now his son Tim volunteers with the Brigade. "In honor of Pa I went and got this tattoo," Tim said. The artwork plays on his dad's nickname, "Mickey Mouse," and the infamous "Old Blue" saw he used to cut holes for so many years.

Right: Tom Schneider proudly shows off his tattoo. The star below the sturgeon marks the location of his home on Lake Winnebago. Schneider has been sturgeon spearing his whole life, and he's quick to admit it's his favorite outdoor activity. "It beats deer hunting any day," he said.

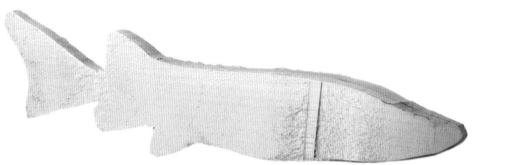

The Decoy

Archaeological evidence suggests the first decoys used to attract sturgeon were carved from mussel shells by Native Americans. When metalworking became more common among tribes, most decoys were carved out of wood and weighted with lead.[2] Many of them today are still created this way, and over the past twenty years, hand-carved sturgeon decoys have become a sought-after collector's item.

"Sturgeon are curious fish," said Bill McAloon of Oshkosh. A good friend of his once worked as a diver when a pipeline was being laid under the river in Oshkosh. Apparently, the light given off by the welding torch he used was a big attention-getter. His friend would tell how he would be welding underwater and huge sturgeon would swim up to him, giving a little nudge every now and then. "He said it was quite frightening to be thinking you're all alone down there in twenty feet of water, and—all of a sudden—this fish would come right alongside you."

It's this curious nature of sturgeon that makes the decoy such a critical component of spearing. Because sturgeon are primarily bottom-dwellers, something is needed to draw them up closer to the water's surface so they can be speared more easily. Although many decoys are designed to look like fish, they're not meant to bait sturgeon with promises of a free lunch. The primary purpose of any decoy—also known as a "coaxer"—is to be interesting enough to persuade a sturgeon to take a closer look.

McAloon uses a decoy carved by his father, for sentimental reasons. He's seen other people use corncobs, wine bottles, and even a dead rabbit in a basket. Because sturgeon live so long, many of them have probably seen it all, and even though most spearers have their favorite decoys, they're usually open to trying something novel, just to appeal to the sturgeon's curiosity. Copper-colored gelatin mold pans were all the rage for a while, and anything shiny—a pail or a beer can—will do in a pinch. Andy Horn of St. Cloud even claims to have attracted sturgeon by dangling various women's undergarments in the water. One can only wonder what all those soggy unmentionables must look like to the fish cruising along below the ice.

Those who prefer to stick to more traditional wood decoys still have a wide selection to choose from. Most are between ten and fifteen inches, but some stretch to a couple feet. The larger decoy helps a spearer identify a legal fish—one that is three feet or longer. The sturgeon-spearing season can be short—sometimes only a few days—leaving the rest of the winter for some talented spearers to simply contemplate their sport as they whittle away at a piece of scrap wood. Carved wooden decoys from the Lake Winnebago region have become an identifiable art form, and many carvers design them to be pleasing to their own eyes, not just to the eyes of a sturgeon.

Three of George Schmidt's decoys show the stages of the carving process from a rough piece of wood to a finished work of art.

Frank Denslow carved these two decoys at least sixty years ago. Denslow was a member of the Stockbridge Indian Tribe, a community of Mohican Indians who once lived on the east shore of Lake Winnebago. Both decoys now belong to the Burg family of Stockbridge. Don Burg remembered that the Stockbridge Indians would usually spear in March, when temperatures were milder and the ice was easier to chop through. They also lay flat on their stomach to have a better view though the ice hole, a practice that Burg used successfully during his sixty years of spearing.

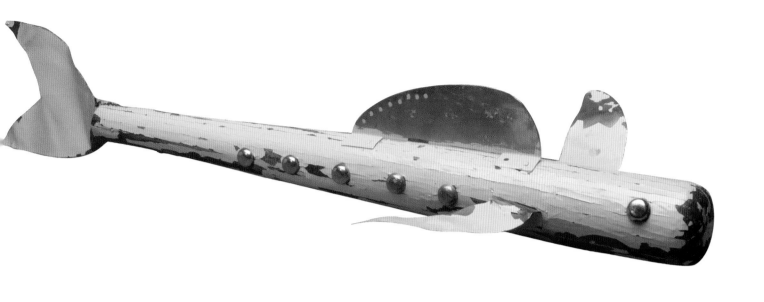

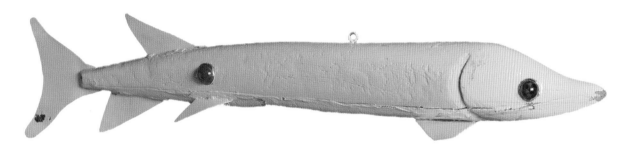

Baseball bat decoy, Artist: Unknown, early 1940s, 24 inches long

Yellow decoy with fins made from license plate and bicycle reflectors for eyes, Artist: Linus Venne, early 1940s, 22 inches long

Red and yellow decoy, Artist: Ambrose Langenfeld, early 1950s, 14 inches long

George Schmidt, Appleton, Wisconsin

George Schmidt is a sturgeon decoy carver who has never speared a sturgeon. He carved his first decoy in 1955, as a favor to his boss. He uses basswood and pine usually, because they're easier to carve. However, they're also more buoyant and require more lead to weigh them down.

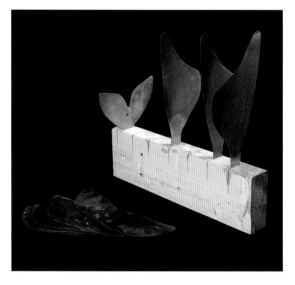

Schmidt said he takes a lot of pride in carving a decoy that a spearer enjoys using. He donates most of his decoys to be used as fund-raisers for groups such as Ducks Unlimited, Trout Unlimited, and Sturgeon For Tomorrow.

"I enjoy making them," he said. "You know, it's not the profit. I enjoy when someone says 'Hey, I got my sturgeon with George's decoy, and now my buddy wants one, too.'"

Weaker(?) Sex
Proves Best at
Fish Spearing

St. Peter, Wis. — Women
aren't taking a back seat to
the men when it comes to
spearing sturgeon this season.
Mrs. Mary Lou Schneider reported taking a 107 pound, 6
feet sturgeon from Lake Winnebago this week. Mrs. Schneider, 5-4 and 115 pounds, landed
the 72 inch fish within a half
hour.

Mary Lou Schneider, Taycheedah, Wisconsin

The first decoy Mary Lou Schneider made was from a bowling pin she got from the local bowling alley. She decorated it and plopped it in the hole, and thirty minutes later she speared a 107-pound sturgeon.

It was her largest but not her first. As a girl, Schneider sat with her father in his shanty, and she speared her first sturgeon when she was sixteen.

Since her bowling pin adventures, she has gone on to create more traditional decoys. The process starts at the wood pile in her barn and ends with a couple dozen brightly painted fish, many of which are snapped up by admirers over the winter.

Schneider shared her art form as a tribute to Wisconsin's 150 years of statehood during the 1998 Smithsonian Folklife Festival. She and her brother Bill Casper towed their shanties out to Washington, D.C., to showcase the spearing tradition and answer questions from curi-ous—sometimes perplexed—passersby. "When you tell them you drive on the lake with your truck, they can't believe that," said Schneider during the two-week exhibition.

Above: A variety of sturgeon decoys made by Mary Lou Schneider.

Mike Laack purchased this striking decoy made by Eric Oleson, and he's had good luck with it. "The copper color brightens up the hole and attracts the sturgeon," he said. One of Mary Lou Schneider's decoys dangles below.

Vern Gebhart, Hilbert, Wisconsin

When his eighty-year-old friend Jake Schroven retired from decoy carving, Vern Gebhart decided to take it up. His first decoy was from a plain piece of wood, so he crafted his own wood-burning designs to decorate it. Since then, he has experimented with thirty-five different types of woods to produce some very imaginative decoys.

"Every piece of wood is different," said Gebhart. "I thought I would make a decoy from every type of wood I could think of, but I gave up on that." He abandoned the idea because someone told him there are four thousand varieties of domestic wood.

Gebhart and his wife, Karla, burn firewood to heat their farmhouse, and soon Karla began rescuing interesting bits from the woodpile to fuel her husband's new hobby. A striking knot in the fiber will produce a beautiful adornment, or a bent piece of wood will give the decoy a natural sense of movement.

Decoy carving is a time-consuming process, taking between six and twenty-six hours to complete each one. Nonetheless, Gebhart has managed to fill the house up with wooden fish. "I keep asking him when he's going to start dusting them," Karla said.

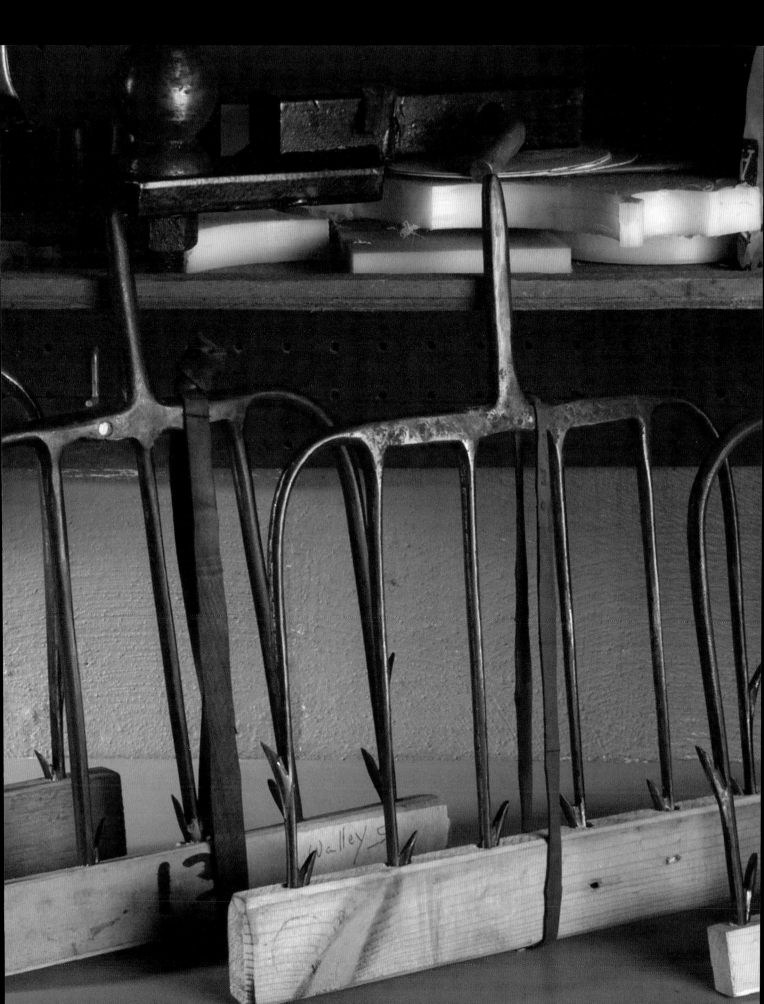

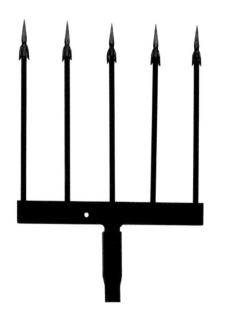

Sturgeon spear with "flying barbs"
Artist: Art Sonnenberg

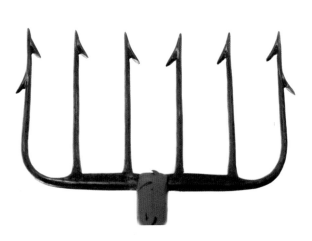

Sturgeon spear
Artist: John Jurgensen

Sturgeon spear with "flying barbs"
Artist: James Nadler

Sturgeon spear
Artist: Anton "Tony" Nadler (1881–1959)

The Spear

It's easy to get caught up in the festivities that surround the spearing season. Taverns put up "Welcome Spearers" signs and order a couple extra barrels of beer, while parents haul their bundled-up children to the registration stations to see the frozen fish. But one look at a sturgeon spear quickly brings things into perspective: this is a primal battle between human and beast.

Sturgeon spears are all made locally—you won't find one at a nationwide sporting store. Each is handmade by someone who loves the sport and is handy at welding. Typical spears weigh anywhere from twelve to twenty-five pounds and cost $150 to $200. Most are six to nine feet long, with a weighted wood or metal handle and a spearhead made up of three to eight barbed tines. A sturgeon spear looks like a spiffed-up pitchfork that's ready for some serious business.

Inside the shanty, the spear is hung from a headless nail above the hole so that the tines are submerged in the water. This placement is very important when it comes time to move into position to throw—the spear needs to slide off the nail easily and without causing any splashing or ripples in the water. The spearhead is connected to a rope that's tied to something secure in the shanty. Sturgeon spears have detachable heads, so that once a sturgeon is speared the handle can be set aside and the fish can be pulled in by the rope.

Throwing at and missing a sturgeon will likely generate a long string of curses and is every spearer's worst nightmare. A close runner-up is hitting the sturgeon but watching it slip off the spear and swim away. To prevent this from happening, small barbs are welded onto the main tines. Opinions differ on whether traditional fixed barbs or more recently developed "flying" barbs work best. Flying barbs are loose and flush to the tine when entering the flesh but then open up once inside to hold the fish to the spear. Either way, a good spear will slice through the water quickly and accurately, secure the fish, and bear the weight of the sturgeon as it's hauled out of the hole.[3]

Art Sonnenberg, Van Dyne, Wisconsin

Art Sonnenberg was born in the town of Friendship in 1916, and he has been sturgeon spearing since the first season in 1932. Back then, his preferred decoy was two corn-cobs with a bolt between them, and he speared with a crudely converted manure fork.

He started making his own spears and decoys in the 1960s, and he still sells both today. In the early days, he charged $25 for a spear. Today they sell for $150. He said he has sold close to a thousand of them over the years, to people all over the country.

Sonnenberg carves many decoys in the shape of garfish, because he believes sturgeon are attracted to them. But other shapes and some of the colors are more aesthetic than practical. "Something for the people to look at, I guess, more than the sturgeon," he said.

These undated postcards show that homemade spears were used to spear other fish besides sturgeon, including suckers.

John Jurgenson, Neenah, Wisconsin

John Jurgenson has lived in Neenah, Wisconsin, his entire life, and he began making sturgeon spears as a child by helping his father. He said he usually starts the process with the spearhead.

"I like to make them out of old forks," he said, referring to pitchforks used for hay. "Old ones—not the new ones, because they have a different diameter." Jurgenson prefers his spears to have narrow tines so they can easily pierce through the sturgeon's tough, leathery skin.

Jurgenson said he cuts the tines off so that they measure about seven inches, and then he heats up the metal so he can pound the tines straight. About half of the spear handle is made from a steel pipe, and the rest is wood. He weighs down the steel portion, which is attached to the spearhead, by filling it with about five pounds of melted lead. "You got to keep that spear so it wants to go where you throw it," he said.

James Nadler, Stockbridge, Wisconsin

James Nadler is a third-generation spear maker from Stockbridge, Wisconsin. His grandfather, Anton "Tony," began making spears at a small blacksmith shop he opened on his farm; James' father, Emanuel, picked up the hobby after he retired; and Nadler followed suit by literally picking up the pieces in his father's workshop after he passed away.

"When he passed on at seventy-two, well, these parts were laying around, so I thought I'd just assemble what he had laying there," he said. "And then, well, I made some parts myself, and just kept on making and assembling."

Nadler estimates he's made more than one hundred spears, and he said the design has improved with each generation of his family. He recently was able to locate and purchase a spear made by his grandfather. "Now, what are the chances of finding that spear after [seventy] years, and being able to buy it?" he said. Nadler plans to pass on the family heirloom to his sons Tim and Scott, whom he hopes will become the fourth generation of Nadler spear makers.

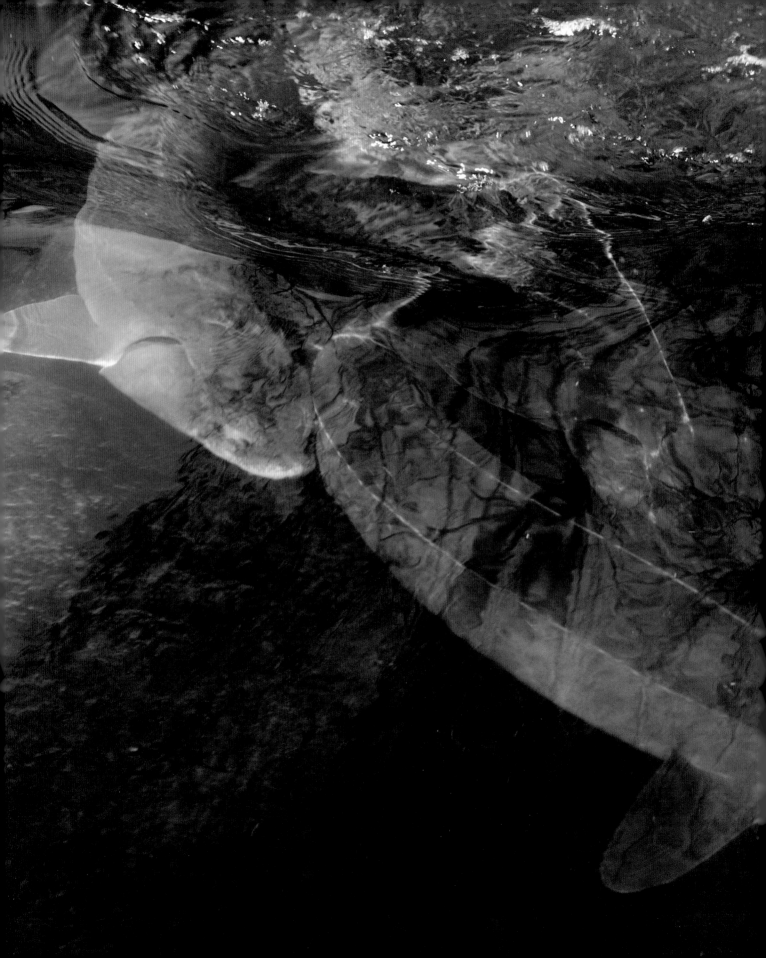

STURGEON FOR
TOMORROW 5

In early spring in New London, Wisconsin, when the last flocks of geese fly high up in the sky on their way to Hudson Bay, chances are good that the sturgeon are running.

Sturgeon spawning is a yearly event triggered by water temperature—about fifty-four degrees Fahrenheit, give or take a few degrees—and it in turn triggers a migration of spectators, researchers, wardens, and volunteer guards. They gather on the banks of the Wolf River and its tributaries where the fish journey to spawn on the rocky banks from where they themselves hatched years before.

It's truly a sight to behold, and parents and grandparents bring children of all ages to witness the event, flocking to viewing areas constructed just for that purpose. Many of the fish are older than the parents, and some are contemporaries of the grandparents. All of the sturgeon look like the ancient creatures they are—nearly unchanged for one hundred fifty million years.

Their movements through the water are like a beautifully choreographed ballet. Groups of fish nuzzle together, some gently drifting over others, their feathery, deep-red gills waving in the water. It's hypnotic to watch, until several male sturgeon suddenly thrash in the water, struggling to gain a good position next to a female about to release her eggs. In shallow water, the backs of the fish break the surface, and their scaleless bodies glisten in the sunshine as they feverishly beat their tails against the female's bloated belly. It's passionate and wet, and in only a few moments, it's over. The fish return to their peaceful dance until the primal call sounds again.

Crews of state biologists line the shore, netting the fish to tag and measure. They also squeeze out eggs and sperm from a few of the fish before returning them to the water. A team of U.S. Fish and Wildlife researchers is standing by—they drove all day and night from Georgia to be here for this moment. They're working on a decade-long project to bring lake sturgeon back to the Tennessee River, where they died out fifty years ago. They'll bring some of the fertilized eggs back to their hatchery to raise and release, hoping they'll take to their new home.

Five miles upriver, a retired couple sits on lawn chairs with lunch bags and a thermos of black coffee. More than three hundred years ago, the land around them was home to a city of ten thousand Mesquakie Indians, who built weirs in the river to trap sturgeon for their feasts. Today the man and woman munch on ham sandwiches and Oreos, wearing matching caps they were issued early in the morning. They've settled in to stay twelve hours until other volunteer guards come to take

Since the 1950s, state fisheries crews have been netting and tagging sturgeon during the spring spawning run.

A sturgeon slaps its tail on the river's surface in late April. Sturgeon use their tremendous strength and powerful shark-like tails during spawning to discharge and fertilize eggs in the swift waters of the Wolf River.

their place, or the sturgeon splashing in the water move on upriver. They wave to a warden passing by, slicing through the water in a small aluminum motorboat.

Sturgeon have been making this same journey up these same waterways for the past fourteen thousand years. To locals living along the riverbanks, the human rituals now seem almost as routine—they're accustomed to seeing the spectators gathering, the researchers mixing up new generations of sturgeon, the volunteers guarding the fish. It can be difficult to remember that thirty years ago these rituals didn't exist.

Since the end of the last Ice Age, warm spring days are what have stirred the sturgeon and sent them upriver, but it was a group of concerned spearers who set the other rituals in motion just a few decades ago. And it's the success of all of these events, year after year, that continue to ensure future generations of sturgeon for future generations of people to enjoy.

Spearers Unite

"I didn't want one of those 'unlimited' names—you know, Ducks Unlimited, Trout Unlimited," said Bill Casper. "One reporter who interviewed me suggested 'SOS—Save Our Sturgeon.' But my Uncle Henry, a priest from Fond du Lac, called me up after he read the newspaper story and said, 'Why don't you call it Sturgeon For Tomorrow? That's what you're trying to do.' And that's where the name came from."

In 1977, there were no sturgeon in Lake Winnebago—or at least that's what it seemed like to many spearers, including Casper, a machinist who grew up on a farm near Taycheedah, on the east side of the lake. Over the span of a decade, spearers had experienced sporadic success. One year they speared around fourteen hundred sturgeon, while only eight were speared during two other seasons. The state biologists knew the reason for the variability. Lake Winnebago had become murky, a result of agricultural runoff and other pollution. Many seasons the water was just too cloudy to see a sturgeon, much less spear one.

But Casper was still concerned about the future of his sport. Sitting in his shanty that February, in between tinkering with the stove and keeping an eye on the hole in the ice, he flipped through a technical bulletin about the sturgeon fishery that recently had been released by the Department of Natural Resources (DNR), the new name for the state's Conservation Department. In 1974, the state increased the minimum legal size for sturgeon from forty to forty-five inches, and the bulletin suggested possibly increasing it once more to fifty inches, as well as reducing the length of the season. Casper didn't like the sound of that—it gave him the feeling that the DNR biologists were more worried about the sturgeon population than they were letting on. He also underlined the closing sentence of the report: "Once the population is over-exploited, it is almost a safe assumption that the population will never recover to former abundance, as has already been shown throughout the natural geographical range of the lake sturgeon."[1]

Casper came off the ice that winter without spearing a sturgeon, but he did have a new mission—to organize sturgeon spearers and hatch a plan. He quickly printed up a couple dozen posters and took them around to the taverns. A few weeks later, 150 spearers met at the Taycheedah Town Hall. The DNR biologists showed up, too.

Casper's main concern was that if some terrible calamity struck the Winnebago sturgeon population, no one in the entire country knew how to raise lake sturgeon in a hatchery. He had been told that it had been tried several times in the past, and each time failed miserably. The eggs either developed a fungus, or the young fish, after hatching, didn't eat and died.

At the meeting, Casper told the group that "the sturgeon in Lake Winnebago need some kind of boost," and that raising them in hatcheries and stocking the lake was the way to do it. He said he already had an offer to help from Rev. Walter Lang, who had a trout hatchery in New London, and the new group he was forming could pay all the expenses. The only thing they would need from the DNR was a few pounds of sturgeon eggs and some semen.

ATTENTION

STURGEON

FISHERMEN

The legal limit for sturgeon has been reduced over the years from 5 fish per season to 1 and the length limit was increased from 40 inches to 45 inches in 1974 and another increase to 50 inches may be necessary according to the DNR.

SOMETHING MUST BE DONE
TO REVERSE THIS TREND

A meeting will be held to organize a sturgeon restocking program for LAKE WINNEBAGO.

DATE: WEDNESDAY, MARCH 9TH

TIME: 8:00 P.M.

PLACE: TAYCHEEDAH TOWN HALL, HWY. 151, 3 MI. N.E. OF FOND DU LAC

If there are questions, contact Bill Casper at 921-1358. Rt. 4 Fond du Lac, WI.

Above: Bill Casper founded Sturgeon For Tomorrow in 1977.

Left: Founders of the Southwest Chapter of Sturgeon For Tomorrow in 1980—Dave Domboski, Wayne Hoelzel, Lee Patt, Mike Schrage, Glenn Ninneman, Mike Wendt, Jerry Oreich, and Fritz Wendt.

For the Love of a Fish

Members of Sturgeon For Tomorrow know how to have a good time—and raise money doing it.

Their five annual banquets—one for each chapter—raise thousands of dollars each year that help support the Sturgeon Guard program, spawning and nursery site construction on the Wolf River, sturgeon-population assessments, and special assessment equipment purchases. As of 2008, the group has donated more than seven hundred fifty thousand dollars to sturgeon research and management since its formation.

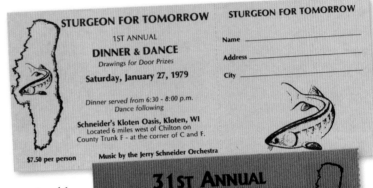

They mean business, but Sturgeon For Tomorrow members also go to great lengths to make sure their banquets are an enjoyable social event for the community. Area businesses and individuals donate hundreds of door prizes and raffle items, and a lively emcee keeps the crowd entertained.

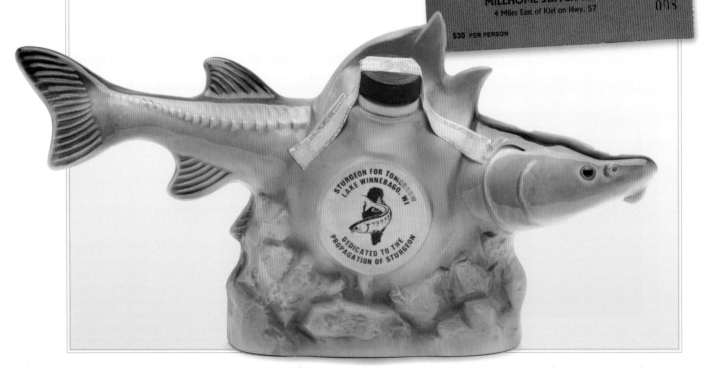

Above: Some of the original founders and members of Sturgeon For Tomorrow's Main Chapter. They are, from left to right: Mary Lou Schneider (founder with her husband, Vic), Gloria Groeschel and Dan Groeschel (founder and current director), Betty Lemke, Dave Vogds (current director and president of the Main Chapter), Lloyd Lemke (founder), Kathy Casper, and Bill Casper (former president of the Main Chapter and overall Sturgeon For Tomorrow, and current director).

Left: Sturgeon enthusiasts enjoy games, door prizes, and a hearty meal at the Main Chapter Sturgeon For Tomorrow Banquet at the Mill Home Supper Club in Kiel.

Opposite page: This special Jim Beam Distillery sturgeon bottle, distributed by Badger Liquor, raised $28,770 for Sturgeon For Tomorrow in 1980.

Dan Folz, DNR fisheries biologist, nets a sturgeon on the Wolf River in 1964.

Dan Folz, the DNR area fish manager in Oshkosh, was skeptical. He stood up and tried to convince the crowd that the sturgeon population wasn't declining and that therefore stocking fish was unnecessary. In fact, he said, what would give the population a boost would be to stop the poaching that was still going on upriver during the spring spawning run. Folz's words reflected a major shift in the way the state now preferred to manage fish, especially long-lived, slow-to-mature ones such as lake sturgeon. The answer wasn't stocking—it was giving them a chance to make it on their own.

Casper wasn't deterred. At the meeting four people approached him to form a board for the new sturgeon group—Bob Blanck, Dan Groeshel, Lloyd Lemke, and Vic Schneider. Sturgeon For Tomorrow was born.

With the spearers organized, and a four thousand-name petition making its way to Madison, tenuous negotiations began between Sturgeon For Tomorrow and the DNR. Casper was now dealing directly with administrators in Madison, and he was frustrated. "We have been told repeatedly by members of the DNR that Sturgeon Propagation is not possible," he wrote to Jim Addis, DNR Fisheries Chief. "Surely, someone in the DNR must have tried to raise sturgeon to know that it can not be done. I am also sure that the reason for trying meant that someone felt the need to restock or assist the sturgeon population in the lakes and rivers of our state."[2]

Meanwhile, DNR staff were huddled up trying to figure out what to do about the discontented spearers—and the elected officials they had started to contact. Besides believing that a rearing program wasn't necessary, many of the biologists didn't think it would work. Gordon Priegel, a fisheries biologist, said that little was known about sturgeon from the time they hatch in the rivers until the time they appear in Lake Winnebago at approximately twenty inches in length. What did they eat and what kind of habitat did they prefer? Others were concerned about the political implications. Vern Hacker, another fisheries biologist, raised the possibility that starting a rearing program would attract attention from the federal government and signal that something was wrong with the sturgeon population in Wisconsin. If lake sturgeon were placed on the federal endangered species list, that would be the end of the Winnebago spearing season.

Addis preferred to stick to administrative details. If Sturgeon For Tomorrow members were really serious about the project, they needed to draw up a scientific research proposal, complete with literature review and experimental design, that would have to pass several review boards before being implemented. The department had spent decades building a reputation of managing resources using sound science, and it wasn't going to lower its standards now.

One might think that requiring a formal research proposal would have been enough to deter the Sturgeon For Tomorrow board members, none of whom had any scientific background. But Bill Casper was a persistent man. He found a *National Geographic* story that mentioned an American researcher who had traveled to the Soviet Union to study sturgeon in the Caspian Sea. Immediately, he was on the phone to the Dartmouth College switchboard to track down the researcher.

Bill Ballard turned out not to be a fish biologist—he was an embryologist. He had traveled to the Soviet Union to study sturgeon because of their unique early development. On the phone, Ballard exclaimed, "My God, man, where are you calling from?" As Casper began to describe the situation, he continued, "You have sturgeon in Wisconsin? You mean I've been going to Russia, when I could have studied sturgeon in Wisconsin?"

Ballard was—as Dr. C. Everett Coop, former surgeon general, described him— "a true scholar and Renaissance man."[3] He even had his own Wisconsin connection. In 1954, Ballard had chided his father-in-law, U.S. Senator Ralph E. Flanders, for not taking action against Joe McCarthy's far-reaching hunt for Communists. Ballard must have been convincing. Two days later, Flanders gave his first speech rebuking the senator from Grand Chute, Wisconsin, and later issued a formal censure against him.[4]

Indeed, Ballard was interested in everything and anything. He blazed trails in local woodlands, propagated rare orchids from seed, and brewed his own beer. After retiring from Dartmouth, he spent his free time pursuing research on ancient fish embryology, which had led him to Russia to study fertilized sturgeon eggs. And at age seventy-two, he was still very game to visit a group of spearers in Wisconsin.

Bob Blanck, the new Sturgeon For Tomorrow vice president, personally footed the bill for Ballard and his wife, Elizabeth, to fly to Oshkosh in February 1978. At a meeting room in the local Holiday Inn, Ballard sat down with spearers and DNR representatives to discuss the ins and outs of sturgeon rearing that he had

William Ballard from Dartmouth College drew on his experience visiting the Soviet Union to write his research proposal (right) for Sturgeon For Tomorrow in 1978.

to

Dept Nat Res.

James T Addis Director [should it be addressed to him?]

Dear Mr Addis

Following our very constructive discussions with you and your colleagues Feb 21, the undersigned Directors of Sturgeon For Tomorrow herewith ~~present~~ present our proposal for studying out a practical method for artificial propagation of Lake Sturgeon, ~~which~~ It requires ~~only~~ the assistance of your department only at the spawning season, for getting an adequate small supply of good eggs and sperm.

Without illusions as to the chance of immediate success or the number of difficulties that will emerge, we assume ~~that~~ from the Russian experience with their sturgeon species that the principal problems to be solved with our species are already predictable, and that clues to their solution are available. There are six sets of these problems, which have to be studied in this order:

(1) Getting usable eggs and sperm
(2) Fertilizing, silting, hardening and disinfecting the eggs
(3) Incubation to hatching
(4) Care of fry until disappearance of yolk
(5) Getting them through the first month of feeding
(6) Rearing to fingerling size.

Our plan (subject to advice and improvement) for each of these is as follows.

(1) <u>Getting the eggs and sperm</u>. The unique accessability of our sturgeon on the spawning grounds in the Wolf River should allow us to bypass the need for hormonal induction of ovulation and maturation. We propose to furnish float cages capable of holding 3–4 males, caught during spawning and leaking sperm, and 3–4 females in obviously ripe condition (leaking eggs). For the netting and selection we

This is a rough draft but in a form they are probably used to. Be sure to pick it over paragraph by paragraph, adding + subtracting until it says what you want it to say. I may be far off base in some respects. Langs can no doubt correct + add details too. Good luck

observed in the Soviet Union. He drafted a research proposal in his hotel room later that night and handed it to Bill Casper on his way to the airport the next morning.

That spring, just over a year after Bill Casper emerged from his shanty on a mission to save sturgeon and the sport of sturgeon spearing, preparations were made for Wisconsin's first attempt to hatch lake sturgeon in nearly forty years.

Stirring Up Sturgeon

One of the DNR's big concerns about the project was that Ballard's records indicated the Soviets killed the female sturgeon and then slit their stomachs open to remove the eggs. Sacrificing a sturgeon—even for scientific reasons—was immediately ruled out, so the three biologists who were tasked with obtaining the eggs knew they were in for a long night on the Wolf River.

The evening of April 28, 1978, Dan Folz, Russ Daley, and Mike Primising put their waders on and trudged out to a spawning site not far from Rev. Walter Lang's hatchery in New London. They succeeded in netting a ninety-pound female, but after they took her out of the water, the male sturgeon that had been courting her all left. Worried it would be difficult to find another female, they kept the sturgeon on a tarp, poured buckets of water on her to keep her skin moist and gills irrigated, and kept searching in the water for one of her mates.

Nearly three hours later, they finally captured a male. Folz, a six seven former UW–Madison basketball center, had the largest hands, so he was elected the "egg man." He straddled the female fish and rubbed her belly briskly to make the eggs leak out. She had only just begun to spawn when they pulled her out of the river, so it was difficult work to persuade the eggs to release. But by 5:30 a.m., they had enough to take to the hatchery.

While Primising and Daley mixed the eggs with semen from the male, Folz took the exhausted female in his arms and carried her down to the river. For nearly an hour, he stood in the water holding the fish, gently gliding her back and forth to help move water through her gills. "Her gills were working, but she wasn't real active," Folz said. "The more I worked the fish, the more active she became, and after forty-five minutes, her tail started moving more, and she started getting more active, and all of a sudden, she gave a splash and took off and swam away."

It was a true testament to the strength of sturgeon, as well as the impression they can make on people.

"All the years that I've worked with fish and different kinds of fish," Folz said, remembering that moment, "for whatever reason, the lake sturgeon is, at least in my mind, the only fish you can become emotionally attached to."

They delivered the eggs to Lang's around eight in the morning. After setting everything up in the hatchery, they sat down to have some coffee—with a little brandy mixed in, to celebrate.

"May 11, 1978 8:40 a.m.—The eggs just lay there. . . . Not much hope for any development. Appears to be a total failure. Much left to learn."[5]

Unfortunately, it turned out to be a little too early to celebrate. Lang kept detailed records during the incubation period, each day noting the temperature of the water and appearance of the eggs. After ten days, a fungus began to develop. In another ten days, all of the eggs were dead.

Jim Addis could have left it at that, but Bill Ballard's enthusiastic encouragement at the Holiday Inn had changed his opinion of the project. When Casper and his crew had first contacted Addis, he and others had wondered if they were simply in it for personal gain—a group of spearers looking for a way to spear more fish every winter. Addis now saw that sturgeon propagation didn't have to be about simply raising and stocking fish. Instead, it could help the department better understand the early life history of the fish—how they develop, how fast they grow, and what they like to eat—all information that would help to manage the Winnebago sturgeon population more effectively. So he decided to support another attempt, this time at one of the state fish hatcheries just outside the small town of Wild Rose.

Addis invited Ballard to return to Wisconsin for the second attempt, and the retired professor replied that he would do everything possible to be there: "I would

Don Czeskleba, supervisor of the DNR fish hatchery at Wild Rose, worked with Fred Binkowski, of the University of Wisconsin–Milwaukee, to unlock the secrets of lake sturgeon propagation.

like very much to come out with a suitcase of embryology equipment, to (a) share in the fun, and (b) do several critical experiments on embryos between the second and fourth day of development, if the luck improves—as I believe it should."[6]

So the next spring the biologists headed out again, this time joined by Don Czeskleba, the manager of the state's Wild Rose Fish Hatchery. Czeskleba was a hands-on manager and one of those types who was always quietly pondering a more efficient way to do things. When Folz struggled again to push enough eggs out of a female sturgeon, he was surprised to see Czeskleba pull out a scalpel.

"I'd seen fish before that had been speared and healed up, so we knew they heal," Czeskleba later recalled.[7] He figured if they could survive the hard blow of a sharp spear, they'd probably do just fine with a cesarean section. Czeskleba had borrowed the scalpel and some dissolving sutures from a nurse at the local hospital. He made a three-inch incision, removed some eggs, sewed up the hole, and the fish swam away—all in about ten minutes.

When Czeskleba returned to the hatchery with the eggs, Ballard was waiting. In fact, he had set up camp.

Darlene Czeskleba remembered her husband coming home that night and telling her about the professor from out east who was sleeping on a cot in the hatchery. "Donnie said, 'Well, he wouldn't go and stay at a motel—he was going to sleep right there so he didn't miss anything.'"

As Ballard sliced a small block of cheese to snack on with a few pieces of rye bread, next to him a new generation of lake sturgeon was born.

Meanwhile, a special delivery arrived in the laboratory of Fred Binkowski, fishery researcher at the University of Wisconsin in Milwaukee. The DNR didn't want all of their eggs in one basket—or in this case, one hatchery—so Addis had asked Binkowski to raise some of them in Milwaukee as an insurance policy in case anything went wrong at Wild Rose. But nothing did go wrong—80 percent of the eggs hatched, and the tiny fish at both Wild Rose and Milwaukee survived. It was the first time that lake sturgeon had ever been successfully raised in a hatchery, and it was finally time to celebrate.

Addis might have been one of the happiest people to hear the results. "The successful propagation of lake sturgeon this year was an outstanding accomplishment

Collecting eggs from a live female sturgeon on the Wolf River

of the Fish Management subprogram," he wrote to John Klingbiel, the department's supervisor of fish production. "Accordingly this information should be adequately shared in professional circles and publicized to the extent practical."[8] Publishing the results couldn't come soon enough—fishery biologists from around the country were already clamoring for more information about the successful experiments.

Bill Casper was pleased as well. Soon after, he sent Addis the first check from Sturgeon For Tomorrow to support sturgeon-propagation research, indicating that "the money is to be used to continue the study of sturgeon fish culture, in the Wild Rose State Hatchery." To Casper's letter Addis warmly replied, "We appreciate the generous donation and your personal involvement in promoting it."[9] In only three years, the relationship between the state DNR and the persistent spearers had transformed from skeptical and contentious to an alliance working toward a common goal. The DNR and Binkowski would go on to unlock mysteries about an ancient fish, and Sturgeon For Tomorrow would go on to become the largest sturgeon-conservation group in the world, with five chapters and more than three thousand members.

The Winnebago sturgeon benefited greatly from all of the attention. With support and backing from Sturgeon For Tomorrow, the DNR raised the minimum fine for possession of illegal sturgeon to fifteen hundred dollars, enough to make anyone think twice about poaching. In addition, it initiated an annual "Sturgeon Guard" for the spring spawning season, encouraging volunteers to help wardens patrol the riverbanks to deter poachers.

Sturgeon also got an unanticipated boost from other events. Along the Wolf and Upper Fox rivers, shoreline property owners had begun dumping large rocks along the banks to help ward off erosion from increasing boat traffic. Larger, more powerful motors were making larger, more powerful waves in the water that lapped at the shoreline and carried away precious soil. The rocks helped provide protection and stability, but they had another unexpected benefit—sturgeon loved to spawn on them. The DNR took notice and, again with help from Sturgeon For Tomorrow, undertook projects to place rock at key sections of the river, eventually increasing the number of spawning locations from a dozen to more than sixty.

But besides funding research, sturgeon guarding, and habitat projects, Sturgeon For Tomorrow had perhaps something even more valuable to share with state managers—knowledge about what exactly was going on in those

The Winnebago Sturgeon Advisory Committee is a group of representatives from thirty sturgeon-spearing and conservation organizations from the Winnebago region who work with DNR and law-enforcement staff to develop and implement sturgeon regulations and management. Standing, from left: Dick Koerner, Don Mielke, Bill Casper, Ron Goldapske, Wayne Hoelzel, Chuck Freund, Dick Mengel, Dan Groeschel, Andy Seibel, Sherman Jacobson, Gary Ninneman, Harry Kachur, Richard Braasch, Matt Woods, Pat Gorshals, John Jurgenson, and Bob Parsons. Front row, from left: Stuart Muche, Bill Marcks, John Buttke, Dave Vogds, Bob Doepker, Ron Bruch, and Patricia Braasch.

PERSISTENCE PAYS OFF

Dan Groeschel of Fond du Lac speared his first sturgeon at age nine, and he had his own shanty by the time he was fourteen. He remembers that when he was very young, his father used to tie a rope around him so that he could be pulled out easily if he fell into the hole.

Today, Groeschel's five daughters are all spearers, and his grandchildren are learning the sport as well. He recently gave his grandson a new decoy to use, and sitting in the shanty with Groeschel's daughter, the boy kept bugging his mother to use it. "Grandpa said this would be a good decoy to use," he told her. Finally, she gave in and lowered the decoy into the water. Five minutes later, she speared a hundred-pound sturgeon. That's when Groeschel's grandson became hooked on sturgeon spearing.

"It's a love of the sturgeon and great family tradition that my father passed on to us," Groeschel said.

It's that affinity for a fish and strong family tradition that led Groeschel to approach Bill Casper when he first described his idea of forming Sturgeon For Tomorrow in 1977. As one of the group's five original directors, Groeschel can look back at the past thirty-odd years with satisfaction—for protecting an important natural resource and for working to break down barriers between the people using the resource and those charged with managing it.

"It's been a great experience," he said. "I think that over the years we've set some new standards for working with the DNR."

Groeschel remembered that early meetings with Sturgeon For Tomorrow and state managers were tense, and there was distrust on both sides of the table. He's glad that everyone decided to stay open-minded and that ultimately they were able to find common ground.

"Good thing we were persistent as we were," he said. "Once we got it going and got the whole program going, I think we broke a lot of barriers, and other clubs, you know, have been working with the DNR."

thousands of shanties out on the ice. For every handful of spearers following the rules, there was one who insisted on pushing the limits of acceptable sporting behavior. One example was the ban on angling through the sturgeon hole.

Waiting to spear a sturgeon can be excruciatingly boring. Many people sit season after season and never see a sturgeon, so it was common for spearers to jig in the sturgeon hole to catch smaller fish and help pass the time.

The problem was that some of those lines weren't really set up to hook an eight-pound walleye. "When you walked into the shacks, and guys had eighty- and ninety-pound test line down, and tremendous hooks that you could have caught a shark on, you knew exactly what they were doing," said Bill McAloon, who helped start the West Central Chapter of Sturgeon For Tomorrow, based in Oshkosh. Apparently some spearers were using baited lines to hook a sturgeon and then speared the fish while it was stuck on the line.

After hearing several reports like McAloon's, Ron Bruch, who had taken over the sturgeon program in 1990 after Dan Folz retired, decided to hold a public meeting. In addition to the decision to ban angling gear from sturgeon shanties, the meeting led to the formation of the Winnebago Citizens Sturgeon Advisory Committee, a group of representatives from thirty sturgeon-spearing and conservation organizations from the Winnebago region who work with DNR and law-enforcement staff to develop and implement regulations and management actions. In a way, it's a scaled-down, species-specific version of the Wisconsin Conservation Congress formed in the 1930s. Since its creation in 1992, the Winnebago Citizens Sturgeon Advisory Committee has worked with the DNR to continually reassess and tweak the spearing regulations to find the best way for spearers to enjoy their sport while still maintaining a healthy sturgeon population.

But of all the changes over the past thirty years, by far the most important has been the dramatic shift in the public's attitude toward sturgeon. Upriver, where people once may have been tempted to snatch a spawning sturgeon out of the water, residents now open their land to sturgeon patrols and grill burgers for crews of DNR biologists tagging fish in front of their homes. Ed Singler, whose family has lived along the Wolf River since his great-great-grandfather returned from the Civil War, said, "The whole culture has changed, and it all happened in just one generation. My kids wouldn't even think of taking a sturgeon—it just wouldn't cross their minds."

IN SERVICE TO STURGEON

Bill McAloon, of Oshkosh, owes his life to sturgeon.

His father grew up along the Wolf River. One night, after capturing several sturgeon on a snag line, he was hiding his catch beneath a manure pile when he felt a tap on his shoulder. It was a warden. Instead of doing time in jail, McAloon's father took the option of joining the Civilian Conservation Camp in Glidden, Wisconsin.

"While he was up there—my mother was from Glidden—and he met her," McAloon said. "If it hadn't been for sturgeon, I wouldn't exist."

McAloon's father learned how to make caviar when he was fourteen in order to earn extra money. He later taught McAloon how to make it, too. He remembers that it was very easy to catch sturgeon when they were coming upriver. He said people used to say, "If I don't get them through the ice, I'll get 'em through the Wolf."

Poaching sturgeon was a way of life for many people, but times have changed, and McAloon is a shining example of how. As a man who credits his own existence to a fish, it's fitting that he has spent a good portion of his life safeguarding sturgeon.

Today McAloon is a director of Sturgeon For Tomorrow and the Otter Street Fishing Club, and he's a member of the Winnebago Citizen Sturgeon Advisory Committee. For thirty-two years, he helped train wardens in Tomah, Wisconsin.

He remembers that when he was young, sturgeon coming up the Wolf River were so thick that it was "like a lumberjack running on logs—that a guy could actually run on their backs." Now people get excited when they see a dozen sturgeon in a group, he said.

McAloon has been spearing for fifty years, and he doesn't mind when the season ends early. "If our season lasts only a day or two, that's fine," he said. "As long as it's here for our grandchildren."[1]

NOTE

1. Paul Smith, "It's What Makes the Great Outdoors Great," *Milwaukee Journal Sentinel*, February 9, 2008.

Todd Schaller, supervisor of the wardens in the Oshkosh area, agrees. "Nowadays we get calls when people see suspicious activity," he said. "Thirty years ago, the last thing we'd get was a phone call from someone trying to give us tips or turn in a potential poacher."

The attitudes of people around Lake Winnebago have changed, too. The early settlers saw sturgeon first as a nuisance and then as a resource that could never be exhausted. Eventually, residents saw sturgeon as their right and often opposed state managers whenever their right was in jeopardy. Today, they realize the sturgeon are theirs not only to enjoy but also to protect. The waters they live along have been blessed with a precious resource that is found nowhere else in the world, and it's up to them to care for it. With their actions today and in the future, they have the chance to make amends for the mistakes of others in the past. In a sense, they have the opportunity to close the circle of a tumultuous story between sturgeon and the people of Wisconsin, where the fish are now something to enjoy, protect, and revere—sentiments different from those held by the state's first pioneers and more in line with those of its earlier inhabitants.

On Patrol

There's something to be said about the tenacity of people who sit on a riverbank for twelve hours—without a fishing pole. That's just what more than three hundred volunteers do each spring along the shores of the Wolf, Embarrass, and Upper Fox rivers. Some are parents with their curious kids, some are ardent conservationists, and many are the very people who sat on frozen Lake Winnebago, spear in hand, just two months before.

Wardens were never able to patrol all of the hundreds of miles of river where Winnebago sturgeon spawn every year, so they started a volunteer guard program to provide extra help. Originally staffed by DNR employees and students from nearby University of Wisconsin–Stevens Point, Sturgeon Guard today consists of hundreds of volunteers from several states.

Guards wear hats as identification and are armed only with cell phones and big, bright flashlights. Their instructions are not to approach anyone who might be poaching but to notify the wardens if anything looks suspicious. Two people are assigned to each

Ron Reinl of Chilton has been teaming up with his brother-in-law Eddie Koenigs for Sturgeon Guard for the last twenty years. They're both spearers, and they learned about the guard program at a Sturgeon For Tomorrow banquet. "It's nice to be out on the river and do your part to protect the sturgeon," Reinl said.

active spawning site, and the twelve-hour shifts ensure the sturgeon are guarded twenty-four hours a day. For more than twenty years, Sturgeon For Tomorrow has donated money to help defray the costs of the Sturgeon Guard program.

Top: Before their shifts begin, guards check in at "Sturgeon Camp," an old farmstead just outside Shiocton.

Bottom: There they enjoy a hearty, home-cooked meal prepared by cook Carol Lee King, before heading out to find their spot on the river.

Top: Warden Todd Schaller provides assignments to volunteer guards.

Bottom: Sisters Susan Daggett of Oshkosh and Gloria Nachtrab of Edgar enjoy a game of cards to pass the time during their patrol shift. Their father Russell Tritt used to spear sturgeon on Lake Poygan.

PEOPLE OF NAMA'O 6

A man sits beneath the forest canopy on the Menominee Reservation.

The Wolf River begins as just a trickle in northern Wisconsin, where it quietly meanders past wild rice beds, sandy banks, and beaver lodges. However, by the time it flows into the Menominee Indian Reservation, the Wolf has transformed into one of the Midwest's most challenging whitewater rivers and top paddling destinations.

From Burnt Shanty Rapids down to Keshena Falls, twenty-four miles of the Wolf twist, churn, and crash through the reservation. It was one of the first sections of river in the nation to be admitted into the National Wild and Scenic Rivers System in 1968, and its credentials likely made the decision an easy one: throughout its course through the reservation, the Wolf runs free of dams or any obstruction, and it is surrounded by some of the most acclaimed old-growth forest in the nation. Immense white pines reach like great pillars toward the sky, forming a dense green wall on either side of the river.

The forested boundaries of the Menominee Indian Reservation can be seen from space.

The Menominee have been the caretakers of this forest, covering more than a quarter of a million acres surrounding the Wolf and Oconto rivers, since an 1854 treaty designated the land as their permanent home. Elders recognized immediately that the forest would be the lifeblood of their tribe. Their approach was simple, yet radically different from the clear-cutting logging practices going on in other parts of Wisconsin. They would begin selectively cutting mature trees in the eastern edge of the reservation, gradually making their way westward. When they reached the reservation boundary, the trees in the east would be ready to harvest again.[1]

Despite more than 150 years of logging, the volume of standing timber on the reservation exceeds what it was at the time of the 1854 treaty.[2] As such, the forest stands as a model of sustainability, one noted by people around the world—and above it, too. The trees on the reservation are so thick and lush that an astronaut looking down on the earth from the space shuttle once commented

on a patch of green that looked "like a jewel," just west of Lake Michigan. He was looking at the Menominee forest.[3]

Indeed, the forest is a rare gem, but it's a pittance compared to the valuable resources the tribe once enjoyed. In the early 1800s, the Menominee surrendered ten million acres of land to the United States. In 1848, with Wisconsin poised for statehood and an influx of new settlers, the federal government decided to move the Menominee out altogether, offering the tribe a small reservation in the Crow Wing River area in north-central Minnesota.

A group of tribal elders journeyed to Minnesota to evaluate the proposed new home for their people. They returned disappointed and resolved to resist removal. Oshkosh, leader of the Menominee Bear Clan, was concerned that the land was located between two warring tribes—the Sioux and the Chippewa. In addition to this threat to his people's safety, Oshkosh also viewed the boggy region as a poor replacement for the bounties of their native land. His interpreter later recounted his opinions: "He preferred, he said, a home somewhere in Wisconsin, for the poorest region in Wisconsin was better than that of the Crow Wing."[4]

Tribal leaders headed to Washington, D.C., to negotiate, and in the meantime the scattered bands of Menominee packed their belongings into canoes. From the Lower Fox River, Upper Wisconsin River, and Lake Poygan they paddled to Keshena Falls on the Wolf River.[5] The waterfall was the first place on the Wolf where it was necessary to disembark from their boats and portage. Two years later, it was the site where the Treaty of 1854 was signed, establishing the Menominee Reservation.

It was their new official home, but the area around Keshena Falls was familiar territory to the Menominee people. They had hunted and fished there for years. For the most part, the land was blanketed by a thick, dense forest, with a few clearings on either side of the falls to experiment with farming. Outside the reservation boundary, just a short distance southeast, wild rice grew in Shawano Lake.[6]

And every spring, when the high water beat down on the rocks below the falls like a ceremonial drum, it called to the sturgeon—Namaʼo in Menominee—over a hundred miles downriver in Lake Winnebago. The drum called, and the sturgeon came—masses of tails, backs, and snouts thrashing in the rapids, clogging the river at the foot of Keshena Falls like a raucous, leathery logjam.

Oshkosh, leader of the Menominee Bear Clan, resisted efforts by the federal government to move the Menominee tribe to Minnesota. The tribe managed to stay on a small portion of their native land along the Wolf River in Wisconsin.

Previous page: Sturgeon spawn in the rapids below the dam in Shawano.

Postcard of Route 55 on the Menominee Indian Reservation, Dells of Wolf River.

Territories Prior to 1854 Treaty

Ojibwe

Menominee

Ho-Chunk

Potawatomi

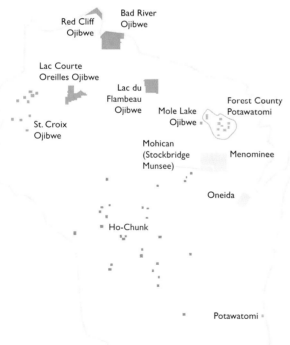

Red Cliff Ojibwe

Bad River Ojibwe

Lac Courte Oreilles Ojibwe

Lac du Flambeau Ojibwe

St. Croix Ojibwe

Mole Lake Ojibwe

Forest County Potawatomi

Mohican (Stockbridge Munsee)

Menominee

Oneida

Ho-Chunk

Potawatomi

Reservations Today

Menominee tribal member Katie Pocan spearing northern pike at Keshena Falls in April 2009.

The Ancient Ones

The Menominee have been people of the sturgeon for thousands of years. They call themselves Kiash Matchitiwuk, or "the Ancient Ones." Among the oldest inhabitants of present-day Wisconsin, their ancestral homeland stretched from Lake Michigan to the Mississippi River, where they lived along the same waters where sturgeon swam and spawned. The name given to them by other tribes, *Menominee* or *Omaegnomenewak*, links them to wild rice, an important food staple gathered by the tribe every fall. But it was the rich, buttery meat of the sturgeon they speared that often saved them from starvation.

The Menominee speared sturgeon during the winter, and as all ice spearers know, they were constantly at the mercy of the weather—whether it was bitterly cold or unusually mild. For the Menominee, who pursued the sturgeon as a significant source of protein to sustain them, the stakes were very high. In February of 1824, John Lawe, a British fur trader living at Green Bay, wrote that the mild winter that year had prevented the bay from freezing and left the Menominee in dire straits:

> [T]he Winter has been so Open & mild this Year that the Lake is not yet taken to this Day so that there has not been a single Speared Sturgeon has been brought to the Bay this Year, the Indians is all a Starving & it is quite a famine for them.[7]

After spending the winter trying to coax a single sturgeon with a decoy through a hole in the ice, the spring—when hundreds of sturgeon swam upriver and could be easily taken—was truly a time to celebrate. Individual bands of Menominee who had been scattered in winter hunting camps came together at the riverbanks and worked together to harvest the fish.

One year, Father Louis André, a Jesuit missionary, turned the annual spawning run into an opportunity to convert one of the Menominee bands to Christianity. In 1673 the sturgeon were late moving into the Menominee River from Green Bay, and the tribe had erected a banner to the sun—which they told André was "the master of life and of fishing, the dispenser of all things"—in hopes that the sturgeon would appear in the river. André convinced the tribe to replace the sun banner with a crucifix, and the next morning, sturgeon filled the river. He reported that the Menominee were "delighted," and they said to him, "Now we see very well that the Spirit who has made all is the one who feeds us. Take courage; teach us to pray, so that we may never feel hunger."[8]

The first Europeans who came to settle in present-day Wisconsin also took notice of the importance of the spring spawning run and how skilled the Menominee were at spearing the giant fish. A French writer, Claude-Charles Bacqueville de la Potherie, published an early account of the area in 1717, relying heavily on the unpublished journals of Nicolas Perrot, whom he had met in 1701.[9] La Potherie stated that just as the Ojibwe people living near Sault Ste. Marie were proficient at catching whitefish, the Menominee were experts at spearing sturgeon in the river. "For this purpose they use only small canoes, very light, in which they stand upright, and in the middle of the current spear the sturgeon with an iron-pointed pole; only canoes are to be seen, morning and evening," La Potherie wrote.[10]

The Menominee continued to live in small bands even after they were moved to their present reservation, and every spring they continued to congregate on the Wolf River to wait for the sturgeon.[11] Residents from Shawano, a town just seven miles south of Keshena, wrote about the annual spring pilgrimage of both the sturgeon and the spearers. J.L. Whitehouse, a lifelong Shawano resident who began running logs on the Wolf River in 1877 when he was seventeen, remembered the scene vividly:

> When sturgeon were running in the spring I have seen as many as 30 canoes come down the river at a time. There was shoal water below the Whitehouse bridge and they would line up across the river not over 8 feet apart and others would drive the sturgeon by striking the water with their spear poles to get them out of deep water. Some of the sturgeon were monsters. The indians at one time hired my father to take a load to Keshena, giving him 4 large sturgeon for pay. I remember one fish that reached the full length of his 11 foot wagon box. I believe that fish would weigh 200 lbs. I have caught many sturgeon that I couldn't raise high enuf by the gills so the tail would be off the ground.[12]

During a journey to the Great Lakes region in the 1840s, Canadian artist Paul Kane visited the Fox River in Wisconsin. This painting depicts a group of Menominee Indians spearing fish at night. The light given off by the torches attracts the fish.

Menominee Fish Dance

For thousands of years, the Menominee people gave thanks to Maqc Awaetok the Great Spirit for the gift of the sacred sturgeon. The sturgeon would provide the Menominee people with food, medicine, and sustenance. The spiritual and cultural connection to the sturgeon was so great to the Menominee that a special dance was performed for the sturgeon called the "fish dance." The fish dance is performed by the male members of the tribe who mimic the movements of the sturgeon as they travel up the river to spawn. The singers on the drum sing the ancient song that has been passed down from generation to generation and the youth dancers follow the older dancers and learn the dance so it can be passed down to future generations of the tribe. The fish dance is one of the main rites of the Menominee sturgeon ceremony and feast.

David Grignon, tribal historic preservation officer for the Menominee Indian Tribe of Wisconsin, leads male tribal members in the Fish Dance during the Menominee sturgeon ceremony and feast. The dance mimics the movements of the sturgeon as they travel up the river to spawn.

On April 20, 1863, one onlooker observed another method used by the Menominee, reporting to a newspaper how they installed a "sturgeon rack" about ten miles south of Keshena at a bridge. "The rack is made of small poles tied together with bark, and put down into the stream in such a way as to stop the sturgeon from going down the river," A. Smith, the reporter, wrote, adding that the large amount of food the sturgeon provided to the Menominee made it easy to "realize the joy they all felt over the big sturgeon hunt."[13]

Indeed, the Menominee feasted on sturgeon, both immediately after spearing them and for months to follow. In the May 3, 1877, edition of the *Milwaukee Sentinel*, the news from Shawano was that "The sturgeon have made a good run, and the Indian camps are full of the odor of drying fish."[14] In addition to drying the fish in the sun, sturgeon were smoked over a slow fire, and often the dried or smoked flesh was pounded into a mortar before boiling with other ingredients. Nearly all parts of the fish were eaten—one historian noted that "a dish held in high esteem was composed of the head and the fins of sturgeon boiled with wild rice. Such especially delicate foods were called '*mitä'o* (medicine) cooking.'" Dried sturgeon eggs were used in many different recipes, including pudding, dumplings, and cakes served with maple syrup.[15]

Phebe Jewell Nichols, who was married to Angus Lookaround, a Menominee tribal member, noted in 1939 that sturgeon was also valued for its medicinal qualities. "Of all meats and fish, the sturgeon, that game fish averaging four feet in length and inhabiting the large lakes and going up into the rivers to spawn was the most sought-after," she wrote. "It was 'good medicine,' its rich oil an efficient battler of lung diseases, and its delicate flesh particularly nourishing."[16]

The annual spawning run of the sturgeon was so important to the tribe that it became entwined with Menominee religious customs and rituals. One elder explained the relationship between the people and the fish:

> When the sturgeon came up the Wolf River to the falls, some sturgeon were taken for a ceremonial feast. . . . Spiritually and culturally there is significance in all Menominee feasts. Like the sturgeon, Menominee live by cycles. The feasts, for example, occurred during the most opportune moment for the taking of the sturgeons based upon the sturgeon's cycle of reproduction. Offerings are always made in the way of prayers of thanks and tobacco out of respect for allowing the people to take the sturgeon. The prayers were to maintain balance, peace and harmony in their environment and in nature.[17]

Menominee Clans

The Menominee are unique among the tribes living in Wisconsin today in that their creation story places their origin at the mouth of the Menominee River, only sixty miles away from their present reservation. This is where their five clans—ancestral Bear, Eagle, Wolf, Moose, and Crane—were created. The clans became the foundation of the tribe's social and government structure. [1]

Within each of the five major clans are several subgroups. The Sturgeon Clan is located within the Bear Clan and was given the responsibility of serving as keeper of the wild rice as well as the tribal historian. Members of the Sturgeon Clan watched over the sturgeon and alerted the tribe when it was time to begin spearing, and they prepared the feast and led the ceremonies after the first catch of sturgeon. Today, the Menominee people follow the example of the Sturgeon Clan by holding an annual sturgeon feast and celebration.

A man stands in front of Bear Trap Falls on the Menominee Reservation around 1929.

NOTE

1. *www.uwsp.edu/museum/menomineeclans/origintext.shtm*

Menominee artist James F. Frechette (1930–2006) carved thirty Menominee clan figures that are now on permanent exhibit at the University of Wisconsin–Stevens Point. The Bear is the Principal Clan of the Bear Clan, which is made up of the Bear, Beaver, Muskrat, Otter, Sturgeon, Mud Turtle, Sunfish, and Porcupine Clans.

Building dams was big business in Wisconsin. Frank D. Naber, secretary of the Shawano Water Power and Improvement Company, went on to build the Wolf River Paper and Fiber Company Mill (above) in 1894. Four years later, Charles M. Upham was president of a gristmill, general store, hardware and clothing department stores, and the Shawano County Bank.

Dammed

The Menominee had an intricate clan system that organized the tribe and kept its society running smoothly. However, one legend of internal conflict was noted by several historians who sought to document the tribe's past, and it centered on a struggle to control access to sturgeon. Two individual bands of Menominee were living along the Menominee River, one at the mouth that empties into Green Bay and the other upstream. When the lower band built a dam to stop the migration of sturgeon up the river, the two bands traded insults and eventually attacked each other.[18]

The story was part of Menominee history years before the tribe moved to its reservation on the Wolf River. In 1892, a dam erected south of Keshena, beyond the border of the reservation, brought pieces of the legend to life.

Charles M. Upham, Frank D. Naber, and Mathias Miller petitioned the state legislature in early 1889 for permission to construct and maintain a dam across the Wolf River in Shawano for "manufacturing and other purposes." There was a dam-building frenzy going on in Wisconsin at the time—that year nearly forty bills to dam rivers were proposed in the state assembly alone. By April, the Upham bill became law, and construction of the dam began shortly after the Shawano Water Power and Improvement Company formed in 1891, with Upham as president, Naber as secretary, and Miller as one of the directors.

The dam facilitated running logs downriver to Oshkosh by maintaining an average depth of ten feet behind it. It was also expected to supply about five hundred horsepower of energy, enough to eventually power a paper mill that was built on the west bank of the river in 1894. It did not, however, have a fishway to allow spawning fish to pass through the obstruction. No records have been found to show that the Menominee people were consulted about the dam when it was built.

The history of dam regulation in the state of Wisconsin is every bit as convoluted as its fish laws and dates back to when the state was just a territory. The first dam in Wisconsin was built in 1809 to provide power for a sawmill on the Lower Fox River at De Pere, and many others throughout the territory soon followed. Settlements often grew around these millponds, but one problem developed, too—fish were blocked from moving upstream to their spawning

grounds. The newly formed territorial legislature took notice and, in 1839, passed a law requiring that any person erecting a dam on any body of water "affix to the same, a slide, chute, or waste-gate, to be left open at all times, when the water shall run over said dam to facilitate the passage of fish."[19] However, dams were being recognized as an important way to spur the economy, and the next year, economic interests won out. The legislature passed the Milldam Act, which allowed dam owners to build dams on streams and flood the property of other landowners without their permission.[20]

The Milldam Act was repealed, revived, and re-created over the next several decades, while the problem of blocked fish migrations persisted. "We beg leave to call the attention of the legislature of taking steps to compel the making of fish-ways around dams constructed over and across our rivers and streams," the commissioners of fisheries wrote in 1878. "No man has a legal right to obstruct the free passage of fish up and down their native waters."[21]

It took until 1907 to establish a fishway law in Wisconsin, fifteen years after the Shawano paper mill dam was built.[22] In years to come, the law would be sporadically enforced on new construction, but many existing dams in the state never incorporated passages for fish. As a result, the dam in Shawano and another built just upstream in 1926 remained barriers to sturgeon migration up to Keshena Falls.

Meanwhile, life for the Menominee people on their reservation was not good. In fact, they often teetered on the brink of starvation. The soil was not suitable for farming, and the people, used to roaming through vast acreages, had trouble feeding themselves by hunting and gathering on such a small tract of land. The loss of sturgeon at Keshena Falls was another hardship that made a difficult life even more so. For a while, the Menominee traveled off their reservation to spear sturgeon on the Lower Oconto River and the Wolf River below the Shawano dam. One elder recalled, after the dam was built, that "the Menominees were forced to go elsewhere for sturgeon. Families would send a few individuals to the Oconto River to catch the fish and bring back wagons of sturgeon for the people to feast."[23]

But as more land around the reservation was bought up and fish regulations began tightening—spring sturgeon spearing was outlawed in 1903 throughout the Winnebago system—the Menominee lost access to sturgeon altogether. However, they never lost their connection with the fish.

Opposite: The Shawano paper mill dam on the Wolf River

EXPLORING NEW TERRITORY

Don Reiter grew up in Keshena, but he rarely explored the woods surrounding it until he returned from college at the University of Wisconsin–Stevens Point. Today, as the fish and wildlife manager for the Menominee Indian Tribe of Wisconsin, he has a close relationship with every acre of the reservation, including the waters that are now home to thousands of Winnebago sturgeon and those raised from Winnebago stock.

Reiter says his job managing the sturgeon population is twofold—to conserve the fish as well as preserve the cultural traditions tied to it.

"For me, it's really been self-rewarding working with our elders, and also working with this fish," Reiter said.

Research by the DNR showed that about 2 percent of the Winnebago sturgeon population live in the Wolf River year-round, and these were the fish that the DNR and Reiter tried to track down and transfer into the section of the Wolf River running through the reservation. Because this is new territory for lake sturgeon—historically they were never able to swim past Keshena Falls—Reiter tracks their movements to find out where they like to spend the most time and where they might be spawning.

In addition to studying the sturgeon that have been transferred from the lower section of the Wolf River to the upper portion above the dams, Reiter manages the population of young lake sturgeon that have been stocked into several lakes on the reservation. These sturgeon came from coordinated efforts by state and federal biologists—when state crews net and tag sturgeon in the spring, federal biologists are able to take eggs and sperm from the fish, mix them together on the spot, and take the fertilized eggs back to the federal hatchery in Genoa, Wisconsin, to raise.

In 2005, these sturgeon reached a large enough size to provide the first chance for tribal members to harvest lake sturgeon in more than a century. However, the absence of sturgeon in reservation waters for so many years has meant that tribal members have not been able to pass on the tradition of spearing sturgeon from one generation to the next. As a result, few tribal members have participated in the sturgeon-spearing season on the reservation.

As part of his job to foster the cultural aspects of the sturgeon population, in addition to the biological aspects, Reiter holds workshops to educate tribal members about their renewed opportunity to spear sturgeon. "Our season has been open since 2005, but the next step is to get tribal members to harvest the fish," he said.

MAEC MICEHSWAN (BIG FEAST)

David Grignon, whose Menominee name is Nahwahquaw, is the tribal historic preservation officer for the Menominee Indian Tribe of Wisconsin. Since 1993, when the tribe began taking steps to regain access to sturgeon, Grignon has played an important role in bringing the community together to celebrate the Menominee tribe's longtime connection to the fish.

"Throughout the history of our people, we lived in the areas by water . . . the bay of Green Bay, certain rivers—the Menominee, Oconto, Peshtigo, Wolf, Fox—and we would wait for the sturgeon every spring of the year to come and spawn," Grignon said. "The Menominee asked for this present reservation because the Wolf River runs through it and because of the annual sturgeon migration to their ancestral spawning grounds at Keshena Falls."

Once an agreement had been reached between the Menominee tribal elders and the Wisconsin DNR, Grignon said preparations were made for the first sturgeon celebration and feast on the reservation in a century. One tradition that was resurrected was the "fish dance," which Grignon said "mimics the movements of the fish coming upstream to spawn." The dance is now performed every spring during the annual sturgeon celebration.

Grignon said that to the Menominee, Keshena Falls is known as *Nama'o Uskiwamut* or "sturgeon spawning place," and the falls have always had special spiritual significance. Even today it is said that when the spring meltwaters rise in the Wolf River and cascade over the rock cataract, the manitou who inhabits the falls plays his drum to call the sturgeon to the spawning grounds.[1] Now, every spring at the annual Menominee Sturgeon Feast and Celebration Powwow, drums and dancers echo the story, as more than five hundred people celebrate the return of sturgeon to the Menominee Tribe.

NOTE

1. *http://menominee-nsn.gov/laborEdu/historic/sturgeonFeast/historyCulture.php*

Keshena Falls

While they are netting, tagging, and releasing sturgeon during the spring spawning run, DNR staff capture about fifteen of the fish to transport to the Menominee Reservation using a special tanker truck.

Paul Cain "Hainy," Brad Eggold, Dave Bartz, Dave Paynter, and Al Stranz (in back) take a break while tagging sturgeon.

Three boys from the Menominee Tribal School carefully carry a sturgeon down from the DNR tanker truck to a special holding pond alongside the Wolf River. Schoolchildren and members of the community congregate at the pond to welcome the sturgeon during the release ceremony.

Two girls from the Menominee Tribal School remark on the size of the sturgeon released into the holding pond. Throughout the week following the release, students will learn more about the significance of sturgeon to their culture through special lesson plans and projects.

David Grignon, tribal historic preservation officer for the Menominee Indian Tribe of Wisconsin, holds a container of dried tobacco leaves. After all of the sturgeon are carried to the pond, Grignon sprinkles tobacco on the water and offers a few blessings.

Students and community members offer their own blessings, after Grignon has passed the tobacco to them.

Later on, tribal members clean and prepare fourteen sturgeon (one is always released back to the river). Here Robert Perez shows two curious children how to clean sturgeon. The fish will be smoked for a week in preparation for the Sturgeon Feast and Celebration Powwow.

In late April, the Menominee Tribe celebrates the return of sturgeon with a feast and powwow. Hundreds of people enjoy a meal that includes sturgeon prepared in several traditional dishes, and they celebrate with drumming and dancing. A special "Fish Dance" mimics the movements of sturgeon as they battle their way upstream to spawn. Here, Bill Waubanascum of Neopit and Eugene Webster Jr. of Green Bay take a break from dancing during the powwow.

The Woodland Bowl is an outdoor natural amphitheater where the Sturgeon Feast and Powwow was first renewed in 1993.

Merissa Bloedorn of Tigerton gracefully jumps and spins during a fancy shawl dance, which mimics butterflies in flight. She is a member of the Gii Taáse Singers, an intertribal drum group.

Opposite page: Tony Fish Sr. of Superior lowers his head while performing a northern traditional dance. The paw print on his left arm illustrates that he is a member of the Menominee Bear Clan.

Bill Waubanascum is a member of the Beaver Lodge drum group, one of several groups that participate in the sturgeon powwow.

Opposite page: Cami Perez, age twelve, casts a shy look at a friend moments before she performs a hoop dance during the Menominee Sturgeon Feast and Celebration Powwow. Her mother, Jeanette Perez, said that the girls invent their own movements. "It all comes from here," she said, gesturing toward her heart.

THE SECRETS OF STURGEON 7

On a July evening in 2001, a large group of people gathered at the Woodland Bowl, a natural ampitheater nestled among the tall pines on the Menominee Reservation, where the traditional spring sturgeon feast and celebration had been renewed eight years before. The group had just finished dining on wild rice, corn, and smoked sturgeon, and now they were settling in for an evening of drumming and dancing in the woods. Some were members of the tribe, dressed in powwow regalia. The others were scientists, policy makers, resource managers, and fish farmers who had traveled from around the world to Wisconsin.

That summer, Oshkosh hosted the Fourth International Symposium on Sturgeon, the first time the scientific meeting had ever been held in North America. After six days of talks and posters on sturgeon biology, ecology, restoration, conservation, and law enforcement, the conference attendees boarded buses and traveled seventy miles north to Keshena. The tribe had invited them for a traditional feast and ceremonial dance as well as to learn about the sturgeon-restoration efforts under way on the reservation.

"The way we look at it," said the tribe's vice chairman as he welcomed the group, "all you people here are people of the sturgeon, just like we are—concerned about the sturgeon."[1]

The scent of fir and the sound of a beating drum made the evening a respite from some of the troubling topics discussed earlier that week at the symposium. On the opposite side of the globe, the giant cousins of the Winnebago sturgeon were in trouble. The population of beluga sturgeon, source of the most sought-after caviar in the world, had dropped by about 90 percent over the previous two decades due to destroyed spawning sites, pollution, and the end of strict caviar regulation that came with the fall of the Soviet Union. A few weeks before the symposium began in Oshkosh, the Convention on International Trade in Endangered Species threatened to ban caviar exports unless the countries bordering the Caspian Sea agreed to suspend sturgeon fishing for the rest of the year.

Sturgeon experts were looking for some good news, and that's why more than four hundred of them from twenty-four countries made the pilgrimage to—of all places in the world—Oshkosh. They came to present scientific papers

Lake sturgeon congregate below the Shawano dam during spawning season.

Previous page: This ten-year-old Winnebago lake sturgeon was raised from an egg at the Great Lakes WATER Institute at the University of Wisconsin–Milwaukee.

and posters to their peers, but they also came to see just what a healthy sturgeon population looks like.

During the opening ceremony, Bill Casper, founder of Sturgeon For Tomorrow, reminded the group that a thriving sturgeon population such as that of the Lake Winnebago system requires a key ingredient.

"The value of this sturgeon and her eggs continue to increase as the numbers all over the world decrease," he said. "No matter what part of the world you are from, you'll have an almost impossible task on your hands if you do not have the support of the people—the fishermen. If you cannot instill in the minds of the general public the need to preserve, the need to assist in watching over this resource, your job will be most difficult."[2]

For more than eighty years, the Trout Lake Research Station in Vilas County has hosted University of Wisconsin student and faculty researchers. Pictured in front of a cabin at Trout Lake in 1929 are (from left) Chancey Juday, Eleanor Tressler, Fred Stare, Lowell Taylor, Ed Schneberger, Edward A. Birge, and Hugo Baum. Schneberger was a graduate student studying with Juday and Birge, founders of the modern science of limnology. In 1941, Schneberger and Lowell Woodbury conducted the first significant assessment of sturgeon-spearing harvest on Lake Winnebago.

It was a lesson that Wisconsin researchers and managers had learned well. Since the late 1930s, when sturgeon spearers demanded that their sport's regulations be based on science, not assumptions, sturgeon research and management have gone hand in hand. For more than sixty years, Wisconsin managers and scientists have been studying the Winnebago sturgeon, trying to learn the secrets of their habits and life history. These nuggets of information have been translated directly into more effective regulations and along the way have made Wisconsin an internationally known center of sturgeon rehabilitation and research.

Starting with the Basics

When the Winnebago spearers rose up in 1939 and pointed out the lack of scientific studies on sturgeon, they were voicing a concern that had been raised for years within the Conservation Commission. Edward A. Birge, who was a conservation commissioner for many years and later went on to be president of the University of Wisconsin–Madison, wrote in 1912 that one of the biggest obstacles to establishing effective fish regulations in the state was that "the state has not at hand sufficient knowledge on which to base its regulations."[3]

Some of the very first research on sturgeon in Wisconsin was directed toward trying to find a way to raise them in a hatchery. After all, that's what the state had been doing with all sorts of other fish species since 1874. In 1936, Conservation Director H.W. MacKenzie led an effort to explore artificial propagation of sturgeon, asking his staff to find out where sturgeon could be netted in the spring and whether anyone else had been successful raising them in hatcheries. Through Birge and another professor at the University of Wisconsin, Chancey Juday, MacKenzie secured a report from the University of Toronto. Professor William Harkness had given artificial propagation a try, and it didn't go well—all of the young fish died by the time they were one inch long.

In his report of the attempt, Harkness concluded, quite bluntly, that trying to save sturgeon by raising them in hatcheries was not a good plan. "In my estimation the sturgeon can never be brought back," he wrote. "Why not let these people that have been partly instrumental in depleting them realize the situation.

If they wish to pay the price in 'conserving the environment' they can have their sturgeon without any artificial propagation, if they are willing to wait 100 years or more for it. If they are not willing to pay the price of 'conserving the environment' then no hatchery or any other method will restore or even maintain a stock of fish as sensitive to environment and as slow to grow and reproduce as the sturgeon of our waters, so why hold out false, expensive hope to them."[4]

With that said, the Conservation Department appeared to abandon the idea of raising sturgeon to stock more of them in Lake Winnebago and instead turned to finding out how best to manage the existing population.

To manage any fish population effectively, two things must first be known: how fast the fish grow and at what age they die. The longer it takes a fish to mature so that it can reproduce, the more susceptible the population is to over-harvest. Lake sturgeon were thought to be exceptionally slow-growing fish, but no one knew for sure. So some of the early studies on the Winnebago population focused on determining the growth rate of sturgeon and how many of the fish were speared each year.

Edward Schneberger, a former student of Birge and Juday, joined the conservation department in 1935 and eventually became the first state fisheries biologist. Based on some preliminary work by Charles Schlumpf, a game warden, Schneberger realized that the law requiring spearers to purchase a tag for their fish was a great opportunity to collect scientific data. He printed up some postcards asking for some basic information—length, weight, and sex—of each speared sturgeon and distributed them with each purchased sturgeon tag during 1941 and 1942. It was a simple, clean-cut approach; however, he also tried something a bit messier. In an attempt to secure a small bone in the ear of the sturgeon that could be used to determine its age, he asked successful spearers for the heads of their fish. About fifty spearers complied with his request, but many others "did not wish to part with the head of the fish stating that they used it in the preparation of a special soup."[5]

At any rate, it was a good start toward finding out more information about the sturgeon that were speared each year. Through these early efforts, managers started learning just what a unique fish population they had on their hands—female Winnebago sturgeon appeared to take twenty years or more to sexually mature. That meant the spear fishery would need to be monitored closely to avoid a collapse of the sturgeon population.

Knowing the age of the sturgeon in Lake Winnebago is extremely important for the fisheries biologists who are charged with managing them. For the past sixty years, they and other sturgeon researchers all over the world have used a small portion of the pectoral fin to estimate the age of each fish. Cross sections of this fin (seen above), show rings that were thought to represent the annual growth of the sturgeon, much as the rings on a stump can be counted to reveal the age of a tree that was cut down. However, Ron Bruch of the Wisconsin DNR recently found that these growth rings are valid only for sturgeon that are less than fourteen years old. For older fish, counting these growth rings underestimates the age of the fish. A small bone in the sturgeon's ear, called the otolith (right), actually tells the true story about the fish's age. [1]

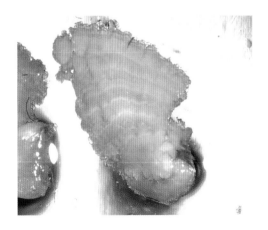

NOTE

1. R. M. Bruch et al. "Lake Sturgeon Age Validation Using Bomb Roadiocarbon and Known-Age Fish," *Transactions of the American Fisheries Society* 138 (2009): 361–372.

Three generations of the Goeser family, from left: Dave, Bill, and Mike

STURGEON-HEAD SOUP

When fishery biologist Ed Schneberger initiated the first scientific studies of the Winnebago sturgeon in the 1940s, he ran into some trouble while trying to determine the ages of the fish that were speared during the winter. He asked the spearers registering their sturgeon for the heads of the fish, so that he could examine a small bone called the *otolith*. To Schneberger's surprise, many spearers refused to hand over the fish heads, stating that they wanted to make a "special soup."

Bill Goeser was likely one of those stubborn spearers. Born in Stockbridge in 1922, Goeser has been spearing and eating sturgeon his whole life, and he can't get enough of either.

"This guy loves sturgeon," said Goeser's son Dave. "He talks about it year-round as far as eating it."

"The best I ever ate," Goeser said. "Boy, sturgeon really is good."

When someone in the Goeser family spears a sturgeon, within a few days the whole family gets together to have a big meal. They like to eat the meat fresh, and depending on the size of the fish, it doesn't last more than a few weeks before it's all eaten. Their favorite way to prepare it is covered in a little bit of flour with some seasonings, then fried in butter in a cast-iron pan. A close runner-up is a recipe called creamed sturgeon—after browning the sturgeon in a pan, they dollop on a heavy cream sauce and bake it in the oven.

But Goeser also fondly remembers eating sturgeon-head soup. After splitting the head in half and cutting the meat out, a soup was made with the meat, some potatoes, and vegetables. Goeser said his family might have learned the recipe from the Stockbridge Indians who lived in the area when he was growing up. His son Dave remembers the soup, too, although not so fondly.

"I remember seeing the soup, but I never wanted to eat it," Dave said.

"It was good, though," his father said. "*I* liked it, anyway."

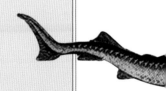

Keeping Tabs on Sturgeon

Throughout the year, Ron Bruch and his crew of biologists and technicians are regularly out in the field trying to get their hands on sturgeon. Their mission is to estimate the size and sex ratio of the sturgeon population, and their findings establish the harvest caps for future spearing seasons. They use different techniques depending on the season, but at the heart of their work is a thin, twelve-millimeter-long piece of copper coil encased in glass called a passive integrated transponder, or "PIT tag."

PIT tags are similar to the electronic chips that veterinarians implant in dogs and cats to help identify them in case they get lost. The tag is implanted at the base of the sturgeon's head using a needle, and it carries a unique number to identify that particular fish. Each time the DNR crew captures a sturgeon on the river or registers one during the spearing season, they wave a scanner over the head of the fish to see if a PIT tag is detected. If an untagged fish is captured on the river, crew members insert a tag and from then on that sturgeon will be known as a unique number. If a PIT tag has already been implanted in the fish, the "recap" will be noted, adding to the information known about the growth and whereabouts of that particular sturgeon.

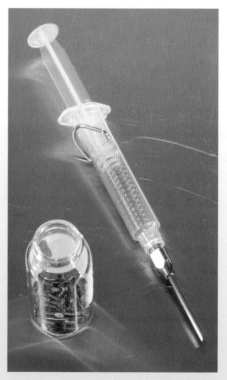

Different tags were used over the years to mark sturgeon for movement and population studies.

Beginning in the 1950s, numbered metal clips called "monel" tags (above, left) were attached to sturgeon dorsal fins to identify each fish. At the heart of the work today, though, is a thin, twelve-millimeter-long piece of copper coil encased in glass. This is called a passive integrated transponder, or PIT tag.

Lee Vogel and Ben Rost measure sturgeon on Lake Winnebago in the mid-1950s.

In 1953, a record season of 2,828 sturgeon speared on Lake Winnebago and the Upriver Lakes caused the first major concern about the sturgeon population since the fishery had reopened in 1931. That year, fish biologists Robert Probst, Tom Wirth, and Edwin Cooper launched a long-range biological study of the entire Lake Winnebago system. "We hope to learn enough about Lake Winnebago so we can wisely manage the waters," Wirth told a newspaper reporter. "Management in the past was centered around restocking, but we have not seen any good results."[6] As part of the study, Probst and Cooper wanted to continue the work Schneberger had begun in determining the age of sturgeon that were speared. To avoid denying any spearer of the special soup, they asked for the front fin bone instead of the head. They also promised to notify any spearer who participated in the study of the age of their sturgeon. The study was a great success—Probst and Cooper were able to examine the fins of 966 lake sturgeon and determine their age. To date, it remains one of the most comprehensive lake sturgeon studies of its kind.

While continuing to monitor speared sturgeon during the winter, Tom Wirth initiated assessments of live fish traveling upriver to spawn in the spring. This was a key step toward accurately estimating the size, migration patterns, and harvest rates of the sturgeon population. Crews of biologists were sent to the riverbanks to net sturgeon, measure them, and attach metal tags to their dorsal fins—the one that makes a sturgeon look like a shark swimming in the water. Each tag had a unique number to identify that particular fish. The biologists also got a hand from the crews of fishermen hired by the state to remove rough fish throughout the Lake Winnebago system. At that time, these nongame fish—such as carp, sheepshead, and lawyers—were viewed as the equivalent of weeds in a garden. In the huge nets they used to catch the trash fish, the fishermen also caught a large number of sturgeon, so the biologists asked them to measure and tag the sturgeon before releasing them back into the water.

PICKLED FISH
À LA GORDON PRIEGEL

Gordon Priegel was born and raised on the south side of Milwaukee, and he began his job as the DNR fisheries research biologist for the Winnebago system immediately after he graduated from the University of Minnesota in 1959. Throughout the 1960s until he transferred to Madison in 1970, Priegel was in charge of the sturgeon-management program on Lake Winnebago.

One of Priegel's most important contributions to the program was instituting the annual 5 percent harvest limit, limiting the percentage of the sturgeon population that could be speared every year. "I figured it was conservative, and I figured it would work," he said.

The 5 percent cap has been used managing the Winnebago sturgeon ever since, and today it's viewed as a standard throughout the sturgeon scientific community worldwide.

Priegel also spent a lot of time hunkered down at a laboratory bench, going through jars and jars of pickled sturgeon gonads that had been collected during the spearing seasons and preserved. It certainly wasn't the most appealing work, but his records turned out to be incredibly important when, nearly thirty years later, Ron Bruch began detailed studies of the stages of how sturgeon mature.

"His notes were so detailed that we were able to take the criteria that we use today for sexing and staging fish, and just by simply looking at his notes, we were able to confidently assign a sex and stage to every fish that he looked at," Bruch said. "It was very valuable information, because it gave us a peek into the details of the sturgeon-spearing harvest in the mid-1950s."

Gordie Priegel, in 1964 (left) and in 2008 (above), still enjoys a good pipe while he works.

Recess and Renewal

With the sturgeon research results from the 1940s and 1950s as a foundation, the state fish biologists were able to establish a series of new regulations to protect the sturgeon population. The spearing season was shortened to three weeks, the catch limit became one fish per season, and spearers were required to register their fish by 6:00 p.m. the day it was speared. From keeping track of the tagged sturgeon that were speared or recaptured, the biologists also had a good idea of how many legal-size sturgeon were swimming around in the system (11,320), and they established a ceiling for the amount of sturgeon that could be speared every year without threatening the population (5 percent).

With the new regulations in place and a slew of data collected, the sturgeon situation seemed under control, and other priorities began to take its place. For ten years, there would be no more assessments of spawning sturgeon, and with the 1967 reorganization of the Conservation Department into the Department of Natural Resources, Oshkosh no longer had a sturgeon biologist.[7] Spearing registrations continued, but the responsibility of registering speared sturgeon was turned over to the local taverns, which was a big help to the state managers at the time, but occasionally the lengths and weights recorded were inaccurate.

At the same time, the Lake Winnebago ecosystem was in the midst of a dramatic upheaval. Nonpoint pollution from agriculture, industry, and other sources had been building up in the lake for years, and its effects suddenly became very noticeable in the 1960s and 1970s. Numbers of macrophytes—the aquatic plants that provide important habitat for fish and oxygen to the water—crashed, and in their place grew algae that sucked up the oxygen and clouded the water.

Cloudy water meant very poor conditions for sturgeon spearing—it's difficult to spear a sturgeon if you can't see it. The number of sturgeon speared every year dropped sharply, and one winter just eight fish were taken out of Lake Winnebago. To be sure, it was great news for the sturgeon population, but the spearers were not so happy. And with no sturgeon biologist to give them any answers about what was going on, it made them downright irritable.

This was the environment that Dan Folz stepped into when he became the new Oshkosh area fish manager in 1973. However, he took it in stride—and at

LIVING FOSSILS

Dan Folz and Mike Primising both started working as state biologists in the late 1950s. Folz eventually went on to become the fish manager in Oshkosh, and Primising had the same position in Wautoma.

When Folz and Primising first started working on spring sturgeon-tagging crews, there were only seven spawning sites along the Wolf River, and they worked around the clock to tag as many sturgeon as possible. Sometimes they strung lights in the trees so they could tag all night, and locals coming out of the taverns would see them and bring back sandwiches and coffee. It was grueling work netting and hauling all of those fish out of the water, but the two men still remember it fondly.

"There's nothing like sitting on the banks of the Wolf River at about 2:30 in the morning and listening, when everything is quiet, listening to the great horned owl or the barred owls cut loose along the river," Primising said. "Or if you had your dip net . . . if you had that laying in the water . . . you could hear that dip net handle vibrating as the sturgeon out there were actually spawning. And it would sound on a calm night, quiet night, like thunder in the distance."

Dan Folz (left) and Mike Primising (right).

Folz and Primising both retired more than fifteen years ago, but they still help out with tagging every spring—what has now become for them a fifty-year tradition.

"When people would come to see the operation or to see the fish, we would always introduce them as a 'living fossil,'" Primising said. "Today, we're the living fossils."

Folz agreed. "That's the thing that's a real irony is that a lot of the fish that we're handling . . . now we're older than a lot of them."

Both men laughed, "So you are looking at a couple of living fossils!"

Berri Forman, DVM, and Fred Binkowski peform the surgical procedure to implant a radio transmitter in an adult lake sturgeon in 1990.

six seven, his strides were big. He immediately reinstituted the spring tagging, and, just as in the 1950s, the state soon had enough data to begin making estimates of the sturgeon population again.

Just as important as restarting the research, Folz made a concerted effort to connect with the public. He began making presentations at the meetings of local sporting clubs, informing the members of what the DNR was learning about the sturgeon and how that information was being translated into new spearing regulations. He had been on the job only a few years when Bill Casper led the formation of Sturgeon For Tomorrow, and after the initial tensions had subsided, he jumped on board the efforts to finally master the technique of sturgeon propagation, teaming up with Don Czeskleba at the Wild Rose Fish Hatchery and Fred Binkowski at the University of Wisconsin–Milwaukee. With the close of the 1970s, the dawn of a new era of sturgeon research was on the horizon.

Finicky Fish

Fred Binkowski had a lot of experience working with other Great Lakes fish—including trout, smelt, and alewives—but the lake sturgeon was definitely a whole new kettle of fish. For one thing, the sac fry (the tiny embryos that hatch out of the eggs) had strange behaviors, like huddling together in dark corners of the tanks. In addition, the larvae (the very young fish) turned out to be extremely picky eaters.

Not knowing what young lake sturgeon like to eat had been one reason for the failure of previous attempts to raise them. In his experiment in Canada in the 1930s, William Harkness described the same situation Binkowski faced: figuring out what to feed these ancient fish. "The yolk sacs were becoming small and so we introduced aquatic weeds with chironomids, stones and other river bottom debris," Harkness wrote. "Two or three days before the last fish died, I saw it take a chironomidae larvae in its mouth and shake it as a dog would, but was not able to eat it. I am rather firmly convinced that the reason our fish died when they did was due to lack of proper food."[8]

Ron Bruch, Wisconsin DNR (right), inserts a PIT tag into a six month-old sturgeon. Scientist Fred Binkowski (left) raises the sturgeon in his lab at the University of Wisconsin–Milwaukee Great Lakes WATER Institute. The fish was later released into the Montello River, Wisconsin, as part of a project to rehabilitate the lake sturgeon population in the Upper Fox River.

Opposite page: Eight-day old lake sturgeon eggs incubate in a hatching jar in Binkowski's lab.

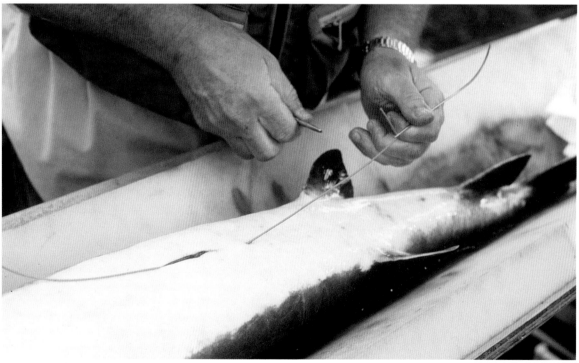

Using his background with other Great Lakes fish, Binkowski went about devising a tasty menu for the young sturgeon, and it involved a lot of trial and error. He tried feeding them a commercial feed made for trout, but they wouldn't touch it. He offered them frozen brine shrimp that's sold in pet stores—no interest at all. He finally gave in and threw in live newly hatched brine shrimp—the equivalent of a twenty-ounce rib eye at a fancy steakhouse. His discriminating diners gobbled it up.

Binkowksi then decided to test them. "So I thought, why don't I take the freshest food—the food that's live. I'll heat it in the microwave, and then cool it down and give it to them, and see what they do with that. And surprisingly, they ate that," Binkowski said. "It must have something to do with the nutritional value or the smell, or something that's still there to say to them 'This isn't frozen and it hasn't been sitting in a freezer for six months, this is freshly killed and I can eat this—I want this.'"

In the following years, the DNR cooperated with Binkowski so that he could collect sturgeon eggs during spring spawning and run a number of experiments to perfect the culturing techniques. He also started presenting his findings at a few scientific fisheries meetings. The first was in New Orleans in the spring of 1980, and Binkowski's presentation was the only one on sturgeon. Following the session, he was quickly surrounded in the hallway by a few other researchers who had started their own propagation studies on other types of sturgeon. Ted Smith was working on Atlantic sturgeon in South Carolina, and Wallis Clark was working with white sturgeon at the University of California–Davis, along with Serge Doroshov, who had recently defected from the Soviet Union.

Because all of them had yet to publish their findings, they hadn't been aware of each others' work. Consequently, they had a lot to talk about. Those discussions continued at a meeting the following year in West Virginia, when Binkowski and Doroshov met for the first time. And the more they talked, the more they learned about the differences between each species. For example, Doroshov revealed that white sturgeon aren't picky eaters like lake sturgeon—they're quite happy to eat

Opposite page top: Fred Binkowski collects milt (semen) from a male lake sturgeon to artificially fertilize lake sturgeon eggs.

Opposite page bottom: Binkowksi carefully pulls the antennae of a radio transmitter through the abdomen wall of a lake sturgeon.

THE SOUND OF STURGEON

Fred Binkowski has been studying sturgeon for thirty years, and not all of his research has been in his aquaculture lab at the University of Wisconsin-Milwaukee Great Lakes WATER Institute.

In 2002, with funding from Sturgeon For Tomorrow, Fred Binkowksi and Ron Bruch began a twenty-five-year sturgeon-rehabilitation project on the Upper Fox River. Part of the study involves inserting special tags into sturgeon raised in Binkowski's lab. After the fish are released in the river, Binkowski and Bruch can "listen" for them to learn where they travel at different times of the year.

It's a technique called radio telemetry. Sometimes the "listening" can be done by boat, but when the sturgeon really start moving, Binkowski takes to the air. While the pilot minds the controls and buzzes over the Lake Winnebago system, Binkowski listens for the faint beeps that let him know one of his fish is below. Each location is then marked using a GPS unit.

Most of the scientific data on the Winnebago sturgeon have been collected from adult fish, either when they were speared in the winter or captured and released in the spring. Listening for his fish has given Binkowski a rare glimpse at the behaviors of young sturgeon. So far, about half of those released have ended up in Lake Poygan, one of the Upriver Lakes.

"There must be something very special about Lake Poygan in terms of habitat and food," Binkowski said. His next step will be to closely examine the areas frequented by the sturgeon to find out what exactly draws them there.

In addition to the young fish Binkowski tracks, there's one special sturgeon that he always keeps an ear out for—his name is Porkchop. He's the only sturgeon from Binkowski's lab that ever received a name, and he certainly earned it. For twenty-four years he swam around in a tank, mesmerizing visitors who came to tour the lab and gobbling up every bit of food he was offered. To say the least, Porkchop really liked to eat.

When Binkowski released him below the dam on the Upper Fox River at Montello, Porkchop weighed seventy pounds and had a girth of thirty-two inches—a very plump sturgeon. He's a legal size for spearing, but Binkowksi hopes Porkchop will have at least once chance to spawn. Perhaps one spring the DNR crews will happen to net him and struggle to bring him to shore.

"They would know right away it's him," Binkowski said. "There are no males out there like him—compared to him, they're all small and skinny."

Porkchop was last "heard" in Lake Puckaway, where Binkowski said he is likely enjoying a smorgasbord of snails, insects, and other fine food that the shallow lake offers.

Fred Binkowski soars over Lake Butte de Morts listening for sturgeon swimming below that contain surgically implanted radio transmitters. Binkowski doesn't normally conduct his research from a colorful biplane, but he would never turn down an opportunity to give his impression of Manfred von Richthofen (The Red Baron).

Fred Binkowski: A researcher's thirty-year love affair with sturgeon.

commercial feed, which is more like the ground beef of fish food compared to the rib eyes that the lake sturgeon in Binkowski's lab were demanding.

Doroshov was hired by UC–Davis in 1978, and even though he hadn't really worked with sturgeon back in the Soviet Union, the aquaculture industry in California was eager for him to start. The idea was to learn how to cost-effectively "farm" white sturgeon to sell its flesh and caviar. Because of his limited background with sturgeon, Doroshov had been a bit reluctant to dive in. "But when I got involved and met Fred and some other people—Ted Smith, and so forth—of course it added to my interest, because I knew that some other people were working with different species, and we were all enthusiastic," he said.

With research programs established on the Pacific Ocean, Atlantic Ocean, and Great Lakes coasts, sturgeon science gained a lot of momentum throughout the 1980s. Binkowski and Doroshov organized a special sturgeon symposium at the 1983 meeting of the American Fisheries Society, where scientists presented papers covering six of the seven sturgeon species in North America on topics ranging from taxonomy and genetics to population dynamics, culture, and management.

In his introduction to the meeting's proceedings, Robert Ragotzkie, director of the University of Wisconsin Sea Grant Institute, lauded the progress made thus far while acknowledging the challenges that lay ahead. "With a life span of the same order of magnitude as that of the elephants, great whales, and even man himself, the difficulties of studying the life history and population dynamics of sturgeon are enormous," he wrote. "Even more challenging is the task of devising and implementing prudent and rational management policies for this fascinating group of fish. Several decades must pass before the results of management practices can be reliably evaluated."[9]

No one would come to understand Ragotzkie's words better than Ron Bruch.

This six-month-old sturgeon was raised in Fred Binkowski's lab at the Great Lakes WATER Institute in Milwaukee.

World Sturgeon Conservation Society e.V.

W.S.C.S.

established 2003

An International Effort

When the Fourth International Symposium on Sturgeon met in Oshkosh in 2001, scientists agreed that there was a need for a worldwide sturgeon organization to coordinate research and management efforts. As a result, Harald Rosenthal from Germany, along with Ron Bruch, Serge Doroshov, and nine other sturgeon scientists from the United States, Germany, Italy, China, Russia, Iran, Poland, and France worked together to found the World Sturgeon Conservation Society (WSCS) in 2003. WSCS promotes sound sturgeon management around the world and has created an international network of sturgeon biologists, researchers, enforcement officials, and public. Since its beginning, WSCS has grown to more than six hundred members in more than thirty countries, and in 2008, Bruch helped to launch a North American chapter. The WSCS has been instrumental in the development and implementation of international sturgeon conservation and restoration plans such as the Ramsar Declaration on Global Sturgeon Conservation in 2005 and the European Sturgeon Recovery Plan in 2008.

Stepping Up

Bruch became the Oshkosh area fish manager in 1990 after Dan Folz retired the year before. He came on board just after the spearing season ended—and it had been a real doozy that year. Over the course of twenty days, 2,908 sturgeon were speared, the most ever taken from Lake Winnebago in one season. Bruch knew that was too many and that because of the nature of the slow-maturing fish he had little time to get the system back in balance. Major efforts to clean up the non-point pollution in Lake Winnebago were paying off—though not necessarily for the sturgeon swimming in its depths. The water that had been cloudy for so many years finally cleared up, suddenly making it much easier for spearers to see their targets.

Bruch was excited to work with sturgeon—a fish he had known since his summers spent on the Flambeau River when he was a boy. He was also looking forward to carrying on the work of Dan Folz and the other biologists who had laid the foundation for the work that lay ahead. "When I got the job in 1990, I was extremely excited about the prospect of working with sturgeon because I had been around these fish my whole life, one way or another—either fishing as a kid or working on different sturgeon crews during the early part of my career," Bruch said. "But then to follow in Dan's footsteps and basically try to fill his shoes—which I think are size 15—was really a tremendous challenge, but quite an honor, too."

Bruch and his crews immediately stepped up the collection of biological data by tagging more fish in the spring and taking back the responsibility of registering speared sturgeon in the winter, to ensure that the data collected were as accurate as possible. They also started carefully analyzing the gonads of each speared fish to get a clearer understanding of how sturgeon develop and mature. All of these efforts led to better estimates of the population size and age distribution, as well as information about the sturgeon that were speared every year.

Managing the sturgeon population was a daunting endeavor, but Bruch was fortunate that his previous job had given him the opportunity to establish a lot of important relationships within the spearing community. While developing and implementing a long-term-management plan for the entire Lake Winnebago ecosystem, Bruch spent much of his time gathering public feedback. The connections he made during that

A QUIET PLACE IN THE RIVER

When Ron Bruch first started working with Winnebago sturgeon in 1986, he was so intrigued with their spawning spectacle that he started taking notes about their specific behaviors. At the time, the only detailed account of lake sturgeon spawning had been written in 1915, and it was just a paragraph long. Bruch wanted to know more, so every spring for the next fifteen seasons he closely watched the Winnebago sturgeon, sometimes spending all day standing in the water with them.

"It was something that we did because we could—because we have such tremendous access to the fish," he said. Standing in the Wolf River, Bruch had the opportunity to observe any of the thousands of fish running upriver, where they are easily seen in the shallow water while they spawn.

Once, Bruch's proximity to the sturgeon was as close as it gets. "At one point I had a female and five males between my legs spawning," he said. "They just about knocked me over." Perhaps an indiscreet moment for the sturgeon, but it was Bruch's chance to answer a longtime question about one particular spawning behavior.

He had seen male sturgeon swim up alongside a female and beat her abdomen with their tails. Bruch wondered how hard they were actually hitting the female, and whether it was that action that released the eggs from her abdomen. With the fish milling around beneath him, Bruch felt the male tails beating only gently against his leg. He also saw a ripple in the skin travel down the side of the female. By standing in the water with the fish that day, he was able to determine that it's not the male tails that cause the eggs to release; it's a contraction of muscles in the female, called peristalsis—the same type of rhythmic contraction that moves swallowed food down the human digestive tract.

In much the same way Aldo Leopold plucked scientific stories from his land along the Wisconsin River, Bruch conducted his research by finding a quiet stretch of the river and simply letting the fish tell their story to him.

"It was really fun work," Bruch said. "I'd be on these really quiet sites, just myself with these fish—no other noises, no other people—and just watch them for hours and listen to the sounds they make."

The sounds had their own story to tell. In those quiet areas, Bruch could clearly hear a low murmering coming from the water, similar to the drumming of a grouse. At first he thought it was the noise of the males slapping their tales against the females underwater. But on closer inspection, he was able to determine it was most likely the sound of the male swim bladders popping as the fish ejaculated.

The sound seemed to attract other males to the site where the female was releasing her eggs. So instead of just one male fertilizing all of those thousands of eggs, as many as a dozen males might surround the female. Dressed in his waders and balancing on the slick rocks, Bruch uncovered another one of Mother Nature's secrets for maintaining genetic diversity.

time eventually led to the formation of the Winnebago Citizens Sturgeon Advisory Committee, which was instrumental in helping to pass more than twenty more restrictive laws and regulations over the next ten years.

One problem that needed to be addressed was that too many big female sturgeon were being speared. Throughout the years, the state kept raising the minimum length for spearing in order to protect the fish until they were old enough to spawn at least once. In 1955, the minimum length was raised from to thirty to forty inches, and it had been raised again in 1974 to forty-five inches. But it was difficult to predict the impact of these size limits because male and female sturgeon first spawn at different sizes. Also, no one knew for sure at what age lake sturgeon were fully mature and ready to reproduce and what length corresponded to that age.

By closely examining the gonads of all of the speared sturgeon that came into the registration stations, Bruch and his crews were finally able to determine at what sizes the sturgeon were ready to spawn: only half of all females were mature at fifty-five inches, while half of the males were mature at forty-seven inches. With that difference between the sexes, the forty-five inch minimum length for spearing was effectively targeting the big females that were the key to the future of the fishery.

The results of these findings led to a new lower minimum length of thirty-six inches, which, along with more than a dozen other new spearing regulations, dramatically changed the nature of sturgeon spearing in 1999. Instead of just setting a number of how many legal-sized sturgeon can be speared every year, the DNR determines an exact harvest limit that is broken down by sex and maturity of the sturgeon that are speared. Once the limit of any one of those categories is reached—and this is determined by keeping close tabs on the information coming in from the various registration stations spread around the lake—the spearing season is closed for the year.

While most spearers hope to someday get that "hundred-pounder," they also understand the importance of protecting enough big females to keep the population healthy. The fact that the season could close the next day, and that many people spend years before seeing any sturgeon at all, prompts some spearers to take a smaller fish and hope for the sturgeon of their dreams to come through their hole next year. The end result: the proportion of adult female sturgeon in the spear harvest dropped from nearly one out of every two fish to one out of three.

Some Secrets Revealed

Tagging more sturgeon and collecting more information about them allowed the DNR to establish sound, conservative regulations to protect the Winnebago sturgeon population. And along the way, Bruch had the opportunity to dig deeper into the data to reveal some interesting details about the fish—secrets that could be deciphered only because of the wealth of information that had been collected by his predecessors for more than sixty years.

Pectoral fins had been used to determine ages of sturgeon since 1916 in Russia, and while they were known to be accurate for the first ten years of the fish's life, it had never been proved that they remained accurate past that age. With so many sturgeon tagged and measured over the years in the Winnebago system, Bruch decided to see if the age estimates they had been making based on those fins were really accurate.

Bruch looked in the database of more than forty thousand tagged sturgeon and found forty-six that were captured and tagged while young enough that their age could be accurately determined by their length. These fish had also been recaptured up to twenty-five years later, and a small portion of their pectoral fin bones were taken. He added to his study some of the large, old fish speared during the winter. To determine the age of these sturgeon, he used Bomb-radio carbon dating of the core of the otolith—that bone in the fish's ear that Ed Schneberger had been trying to get his hands on in the 1940s by talking spearers out of making their special sturgeon head soup.

When Bruch compared the true ages of all of these fish to the ages that had been estimated based on the pectoral fin samples, he found that the sturgeon were older than everyone had previously believed. Age estimates based on pectoral fins were accurate only up to age fourteen—beyond that, they underestimated the true age of the fish. Sturgeon that had been thought to be twenty-five years old were actually closer to thirty, and fish that were recorded to be forty-five years old were actually pushing fifty-five. Bruch also found that examining otoliths tells the true story about the fish's age—a discovery that likely will now be used by sturgeon biologists all around the world.

Bruch created a mathematical model that corrected the fourteen thousand estimated ages in the DNR database, which allowed him to fill in many of the gaps in the data that had been collected since the 1940s. It also gave him the opportunity to solve one mystery that had been puzzling the Winnebago sturgeon biologists for years.

"When the biologists in the 1950s began mapping out the entire sturgeon population based on length, there was a 'hole' in the population of a lot of fish that were missing," Bruch explained. "The medium-size fish that would have been twenty to twenty-five years old—those fish were gone. There was just a big hole there, and they couldn't explain it."

Now that he knows how old the Winnebago sturgeon really are, Bruch has been able to determine that those missing fish hatched in the early 1920s. By the 1930s, they would have grown large enough to be pulled out of the water on setlines that littered the Upriver Lakes during that time. Although in 1931 a legal fall season was opened where five fish could be taken, the season was eventually closed in 1952 because there were so many reports of poaching. The missing fish that the biologists couldn't explain likely disappeared due to illegal setline fishing.

That hole in the population, Bruch said, just passed through during the past decade. Recently, spearers have been pulling out larger fish from Lake Winnebago, and the final disappearance of this hole in the population is one of the reasons why. The hundred-pound sturgeon that are speared today are the fish that started receiving protection from a law passed nearly sixty years ago—an important reminder of how sturgeon must be managed. "It's a testament to how far back you have to look in the past to find out what could have affected the current population," Bruch said. "Sturgeon aren't really managed on a yearly basis—they're managed over decades and centuries."

More than a century has passed since Wisconsin enacted the first law to protect sturgeon from overexploitation. Throughout that time, the tradition of sturgeon spearing and the demand for science-based regulations has made the Winnebago sturgeon one of the most studied sturgeon populations in the world. All of the attention has paid off handsomely for both the sturgeon and the people of Wisconsin—today there are more than sixty thousand sturgeon swimming in the Lake Winnebago system, the largest and healthiest lake sturgeon population in the world. And now, lessons learned throughout the years from the Winnebago sturgeon are helping efforts to restore lake sturgeon populations throughout the Great Lakes region.

Up-Close and Personal

Sturgeon spawning is an amazing event, and many parents turn up with their children to watch. But sometimes the state biologists steal the show. Their main job is to capture as many sturgeon as possible so that they can accurately gauge the size and sex ratio of the population. In addition, they often collect eggs and semen for sturgeon rehabilitation projects around the country. However, they also have a fantastic opportunity to educate the public about just how special this ancient fish is—while telling stories about why sturgeon are so different from other fish, they let the children touch the sturgeon's leathery skin and look at its strange suction-cup mouth. And they answer all sorts of questions—well, most of them.

Kendall Kamke, DNR senior fisheries biologist, is always willing to show off a sturgeon.

As one biologist flips a male sturgeon over, another pulls out a plastic syringe and attempts to collect some of the semen that is leaking out of the fish's belly. At times, the male sturgeon's leaking turns to all-out spraying, and the biologists—as well as some of the spectators—are hit. Some of the parents watching might be slow to put the pieces together, until their children start asking questions.

"What's that?" says a little girl, pointing to the milky white liquid that just landed on her father's coat.

The crew continues working, hats pulled down low on their heads, hoping they don't have to supply the answer.

The father looks helplessly at the girl's mother. The woman rolls her eyes, takes a deep breath, and jumps in.

"That's what makes baby sturgeon!" She says with a big smile and a bit of forced confidence. "They'll mix that with some eggs and soon they'll turn into baby sturgeon!"

Chuckling, the biologists continue with their work. It's all part of a day's work and educating the public about sturgeon.

A DNR tagging crew as seen from a sturgeon's point of view. Hundreds of sturgeon are netted and released every spawning season in order to tag and measure them. Cooperation from private landowners along the Wolf River is key to the tagging project's success.

Previous page: Sturgeon prepare to spawn on the shallow banks of the Wolf River.

On steep banks, tagging crews sometimes return the fish to the river via a makeshift slip-and-slide.

Opposite page: Ron Goldapske, a member of the Winnebago Sturgeon Advisory Committee, and Cory Wienandt, Wisconsin DNR, watch their footing as they haul a sturgeon out of the Wolf River, just below the Shawano dam. "Dipping," or netting the fish, is a strenuous job during spawning season, when the DNR spends long days tagging fish.

Ron Bruch briefs his crews prior to a sturgeon population assessment.

Bob "Hermie" Marin wrestles a sturgeon out of the Wolf River.

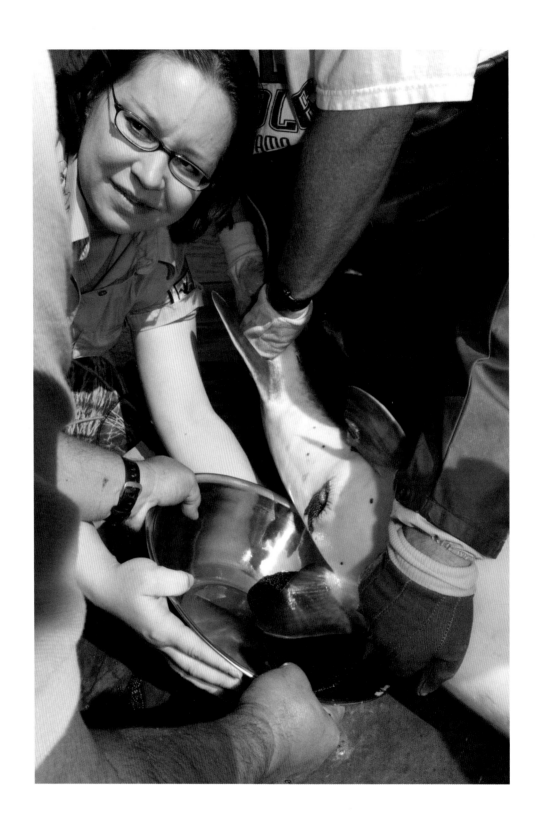

Ron Bruch drives the boat while Fred Binkowski (holding antennae) and Bob "Hermie" Marin search for sturgeon. Bruch and Binkowski inserted special radio transmitters in the fish before releasing them, so that they can track the fishes' movements over different seasons.

Previous page: Jaclyn Zelko of the U.S. Fish & Wildlife Service Warm Springs Hatchery in Georgia collects eggs for the lake sturgeon restoration program in the Tennessee River System in northern Georgia. Lake sturgeon completely disappeared from the system, and the Winnebago sturgeon population is helping to repopulate it.

Fred Binkowski, aquaculture specialist with the University of Wisconsin Sea Grant Institute and a senior scientist at the University of Wisconsin–Milwaukee Great Lakes WATER Institute, mixes up a new generation of lake sturgeon just below the dam in Shawano.

After collecting eggs from a gravid female sturgeon, Binkowski mixes them gently with the semen from seven different males, each in a separate bowl. He'll take the fertilized eggs back to his lab in Milwaukee, where he has been raising and studying sturgeon for more than thirty years.

Depending on the weather and the clarity of the water, the sturgeon spearing season can last up to two weeks. That's why Kendall Kamke (right) makes sure his registration station in Stockbridge has all of the comforts of home, including curtains on the windows and a fully stocked pantry. Ryan Zernzach, DNR fisheries technician from Shawano, works in the warm seat by the stove.

A line of spearers and sturgeon wait outside a DNR registration station. Tim Kroeff, a DNR fisheries management technician from Sturgeon Bay, remembers one winter when he and his supervisor Mike Toneys registered 525 fish in one day at their station at Indian Point on Lake Poygan. "The line just kept growing throughout the day and eventually snaked a block or more down to the boat landing," Kroeff recalled. "One guy said he drank a twelve-pack of beer waiting in line, and I believed him," he said. "And may I add he was very cordial."

Dave Bartz (left) and Dave Paynter (right) make an incision in the abdomen of a speared sturgeon to determine its sex and maturity. Every year the DNR determines an exact harvest limit that is broken down by sex and maturity of the sturgeon that are speared. Once the limit of any one of those categories is reached—and this is determined by keeping close tabs on the information coming in from the various registration stations spread around the lake—the spearing season is closed for the year.

While Paul "Hainy" Cain records data inside the registration station, Dave Bartz, outside, scans a sturgeon to see if it contains a PIT tag, a small electronic chip used for identification. The tag would have been inserted during a spring spawning season, when DNR crews net and tag as many sturgeon as possible in order to estimate the size of the entire Winnebago sturgeon population.

Ron Bruch draws a blood sample, while Peter Allen and Cam Barth of the University of Manitoba take tissue samples from a harvested sturgeon for a study examining the sturgeons' use of calcium during various stages of reproductive development. Because of the unique access to sturgeon in both the winter and spring, scientists from all over the world frequently visit Lake Winnebago to perform sturgeon studies.

Every spearer's favorite part of registration is finding out how big the sturgeon is. Here, Tim Kroeff hoists a frozen sturgeon up to weigh after measuring its length on a board.

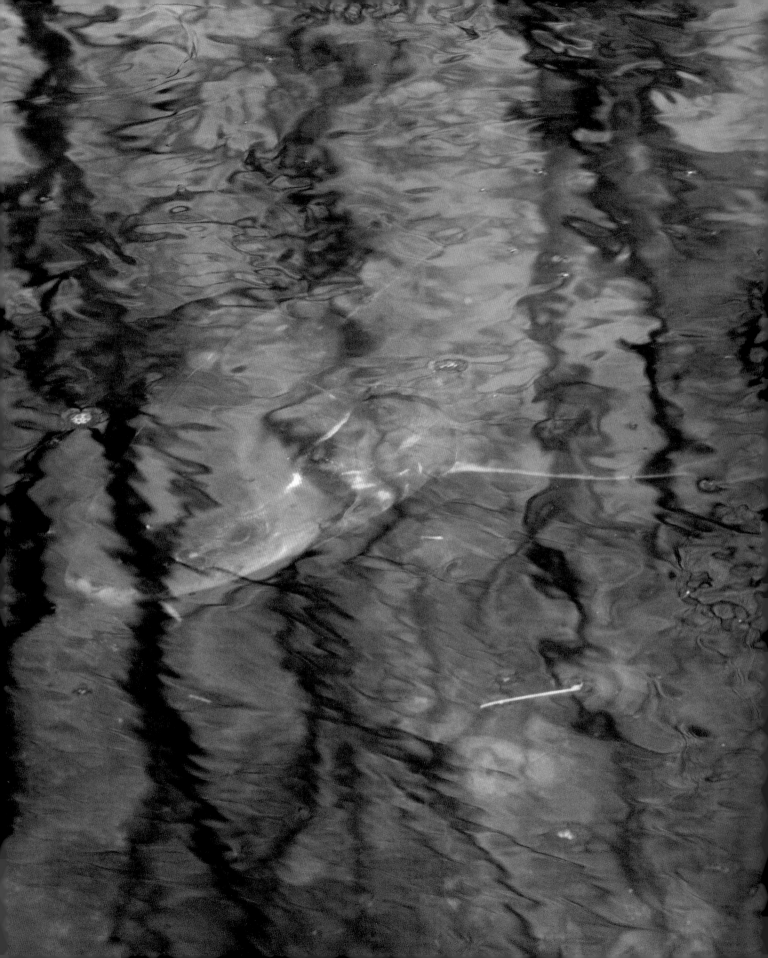

INTO THE GREAT LAKES 8

LAKE
SUPERIOR

LAKE
HURON

STRAITS
OF MACKINAC

Green Bay

LOWER
FOX RIVER

Two
Rivers

SAGINAW BAY

LAKE
WINNEBAGO

LAKE
MICHIGAN

Milwaukee

LAKE
ST. CLAIR

LAKE
ERIE

Chicago

Sandusky

S turgeon seem to inspire stories. They are part of the legends and history of the Menominee people, and they will continue to be part of their future. Stories about sturgeon are scattered throughout newspapers from the nineteenth century, where reporters marveled about the size of the fish and their abundance. And today, on Lake Winnebago, sturgeon are captured in photographs that are taped into scrapbooks by spearers, remembrances of the good times they've had out on the ice.

Even sturgeon scientists have their own fish tales they like to tell and retell whenever they gather together. A favorite is about one intrepid Winnebago sturgeon that decided it needed a change of scenery.

LAKE ONTARIO

In 1978, this sturgeon was captured by DNR fisheries biologist Dan Folz and his crew in Lake Winnebago, just a few months after they collected eggs for the first attempt to raise lake sturgeon in a hatchery. It was measured at forty-nine and a half inches, fitted with a metal tag, and released.

At some point, this sturgeon declined to head up the Wolf River and instead swam down the Lower Fox—the river that by 1850 had been transformed from a series of whitewater rapids and falls to a system of seventeen locks and dams. Down through the locks went this sturgeon, passing by the cities that were once places known only for their infamous rapids—Appleton (La Grand Chute), Little Chute (La Petite Chute), and Kaukauna (La Grand Kaukilin)—and down to De Pere and then to Green Bay, where the French explorer Jean Nicolet first set foot in 1634 and encountered the Menominee people.

It's a thirty-nine-mile trip that drops 170 feet—a significant journey, but not out of the ordinary. Over the past ten years, it's estimated that approximately 70 percent of the sturgeon spawning below the De Pere dam are originally from Lake Winnebago.

But this particular sturgeon decided to extend its journey even farther. Its specific route is unknown, but let's say it swam out of Green Bay and cruised around Lake Michigan for a few years. It may have gone past Milwaukee, where a hundred-pound sturgeon was caught in 1851 and sold for five cents a pound.[1] And then maybe it went down to Chicago, where in 1897 a half dozen good-sized

One Winnebago sturgeon made a significant journey into the Great Lakes.

sturgeon, one weighing 168 pounds, were landed in one afternoon, and the next day nearly everyone in South Chicago was eating fresh sturgeon for the first time in years.[2]

Perhaps this Winnebago sturgeon then headed back north, past the commercial fishing port of Two Rivers, Wisconsin, where in 1906 a newspaper reported that one fisherman had netted a 150-pound sturgeon noting that "this species of fish is said to be getting more scarce every year."[3]

What is known for certain is that this sturgeon eventually headed north, passed through the Straits of Mackinac, and entered Lake Huron. Sixteen years after it was last seen in Lake Winnebago, it was captured in a trap net by commercial fishermen in Saginaw Bay. The fishermen saw the metal tag and reported its capture. The sturgeon was then released and made its way down the rest of the east coast of Michigan, under the Bluewater Bridge at the head of the St. Clair River, across Lake St. Clair, down the Detroit River, and into Lake Erie.

In 1999, it was found dead on the shore of Sandusky, Ohio.

During its twenty-one-year ramble, this Winnebago sturgeon had grown eight inches while traveling more than eight hundred miles through three of the five Great Lakes. It washed up at the very place where the Schacht brothers had built the first major sturgeon-processing plant on the Great Lakes in 1865, igniting the heavy commercial fishing that nearly wiped out sturgeon populations in the Great Lakes.

The demise of this one well-traveled Winnebago sturgeon might seem a sad way to conclude a story about the rich history surrounding these ancient fish. However, the last days of this particular sturgeon in the waters of Lake Erie actually point to a potential happy ending for the rest of the Great Lakes sturgeon population. This Winnebago sturgeon likely spawned before it died, helping to create a new generation of lake sturgeon to repopulate the Great Lakes after so many years of steady decline. In addition, there's a good chance this sturgeon was spawning in a very unlikely place—the heavily industrialized Detroit River.

Nearly 150 years after the Schacht brothers processed more than seven hundred thousand pounds a year of smoked sturgeon, caviar, and isinglass, the waters off Sandusky, as well as other sites throughout the Great Lakes, are showing signs of recovery and hope for lake sturgeon. And much of the good news shares a common thread with Wisconsin's Winnebago sturgeon.

King of Fishes

"Take my bait, O King of Fishes!" So cried Hiawatha down to a giant sturgeon at the bottom of Lake Superior in Longfellow's epic poem. Indeed, before the arrival of Europeans, lake sturgeon ruled as the largest fish in the Great Lakes—and one of the most numerous, too. Today, however, is a different story. In Lake Michigan, based on available data, scientists estimate only five thousand adult sturgeon remain, well below 1 percent of the most conservative estimates of historic numbers.

As seen throughout Wisconsin's history with this ancient fish, careful management is required to protect and sustain a healthy population. Lake Winnebago sturgeon are thriving because of an ongoing collaboration among state managers, researchers, spearers, and the concerned public. It's a story to be celebrated, and it is also serving as a successful model for other areas in the Great Lakes where efforts to restore lake sturgeon are more recently under way.

One of the earliest attempts to hatch lake sturgeon was in the small village of Algonac, on the Michigan side of the lower St. Clair River. A caviar factory was operating there, and in 1889, the Michigan Fish Commission captured four thousand sturgeon near Detroit and brought a couple dozen to Algonac to experiment with artificial propagation.

Today, in that same area, Bruce Manny is working to restore lake sturgeon numbers not by propagation but through providing high-quality areas for the remaining fish to spawn. Manny is a fishery biologist with the U.S. Geological Survey at the Great Lakes Science Center in Ann Arbor, Michigan. He said that although the Detroit River was historically known to support at least nine spawning sites for sturgeon, no one had ever seen proof that sturgeon laid eggs in the Detroit River. That all changed in 2001.

Manny was working with Nate Caswell from Central Michigan University to insert sonic transmitters into adult sturgeon and then track their movements. Two males recently captured and implanted with transmitters were nearly ready

Kim Smith, a fisheries technician with the U.S. Fish and Wildlife Service, and Bruce Manny hold a male sturgeon that was caught on a newly constructed spawning bed near Belle Island in the Detroit River.

to spawn, and Caswell had followed them by boat to Zug Island, a highly industrialized area south of Detroit. That's when a third sturgeon joined them.

"So he was sitting on top of three adult sturgeon, two of which were spawning-ready, and he called me up and said, 'Hey Bruce, can you get me some egg mats in a hurry?'" (He was referring to the furnace-filter mats scientists lay down to capture eggs that fish deposit on the river bottom.) "'I'm sitting right on top of three fish and I don't know anything about this area, but it looks as if they may be spawning here.' . . . So we rushed the mats over that night and set them the next morning, and the following day we had fertilized lake sturgeon eggs."

Since that discovery, Manny determined that lack of spawning sites is probably the main obstacle standing in the way of lake sturgeon restoration in the Detroit River. Partnering with a number of agencies and organizations, he has been working to remedy that. Using information known about favorite spawning places of the Winnebago sturgeon, three lake sturgeon spawning reefs were constructed just off the southeast shore of Belle Isle in the upper Detroit River. Soon after, another spawning area was constructed twelve miles downstream at Fighting Island, a $178,000 project that was completed with U.S. and Canadian government funding.

For Manny and many other scientists like him, it's a very exciting time to be researching lake sturgeon in the Great Lakes. Interest in the region's largest native fish exploded during the past decade, and restoration plans are in the works from Lake Superior to Lake Ontario. Manny said that anyone looking for a good example to follow should look no further than Wisconsin.

"I've seen it from all sorts of perspectives, but these basic elements that Ron Bruch and company have instituted in Wisconsin I think is the recipe for success," he said.

These basic ingredients, Manny said, include a comprehensive research program to lead management efforts, mixed with a strong law-enforcement presence that ensures regulations are followed, and topped off with educational outreach to inform the public about the uniqueness—and fragility—of this ancient fish.

"So that whole mix of law enforcement, biology assessment, and public involvement in protecting the fish and understanding their value is what needs to be instituted across the whole Great Lakes, wherever lake sturgeon are found," Manny said.

Lake Superior

Lake sturgeon completely disappeared from the St. Louis River, so in the early 1980s, the Wisconsin and Minnesota Departments of Natural Resources began stocking the river with sturgeon raised in Fred Binkowski's lab at the University of Wisconsin–Milwaukee Great Lakes WATER Institute. In 2007, fisheries staff discovered mature sturgeon returning from Lake Superior to their historical spawning grounds in the river. A project slated for completion in 2009 will improve roughly eight hundred feet of suitable spawning habitat below the Fond du Lac Dam.

Lake Michigan

In 2003, the Wisconsin Department of Natural Resources began stocking sturgeon raised at the Great Lakes WATER Institute in the Milwaukee River, where lake sturgeon hadn't been sighted since the 1890s. Since 2005, eggs taken from Winnebago sturgeon have been raised in a streamside rearing facility operated in partnership with the Riveredge Nature Center. The streamside mini-hatchery uses water from the Milwaukee River, greatly improving the chances that once released, the sturgeon will eventually return to the Milwaukee River to spawn. The stocking will continue for twenty-five years as an effort to boost lake sturgeon numbers in Lake Michigan.

Lake Huron

In 1995, the Michigan Department of Natural Resources and the Alpena National Fish and Wildlife Conservation Office were able to begin a sturgeon tagging program with the help of commercial fishers, who frequently find lake sturgeon as by-catch in their trap nets. Currently, fifteen commercial fishers tag and collect biological data on all sturgeon they remove from their nets before releasing them. Their efforts are helping to gather information on relative abundance, movement, and life history of lake sturgeon in Lake Huron.

Lake Erie

Sturgeon historically spawned in nineteen locations throughout Lake Erie and its tributaries, including the Cuyahoga and Sandusky rivers, and the Presque Isle shoals near Erie, Pennsylvania. Today, sturgeon are known to remain only in the far eastern and western portions of the lake. Researchers working in the Detroit River area have found that sturgeon hatching in the Detroit River will often end up living as adults in western Lake Erie. That means efforts to improve spawning conditions in the Detroit River through construction of artificial reefs will likely also benefit the sturgeon population in Lake Erie.

Lake Ontario

The New York Sturgeon For Tomorrow chapter formed in 2008 to promote the reestablishment of sturgeon throughout the state of New York so that they may be removed from threatened or endangered species lists and ultimately produce self-sustaining populations capable of supporting sport fisheries. The chapter was formed by Tom Brooking, a fisheries biologist at the Cornell University Biological Field Station, located on Oneida Lake near Syracuse, New York. Brooking is studying sturgeon in that area by fitting them with radio transmitters to track their movements, home range, and spawning sites.

In Michigan, Brenda Archambo is the person who introduces the public to lake sturgeon.

Archambo first saw a sturgeon when she was six years old, while out ice fishing with her grandfather on Burt Lake, on the northern tip of lower Michigan. Suddenly there was a lot of commotion in a shanty nearby, so she and her grandfather walked over to take a look. She vividly remembers seeing the huge fish on the ice and the way everyone who saw it responded.

"The people were so excited in seeing this fish, and the guy who actually got the fish was just almost short of crying—he was so excited and shaking," she said. Archambo was fascinated, and she walked over to the fish and looked right in its eyes. "Looking into the eye of the sturgeon reminded me of pictures I had seen of dinosaurs," she said, "and so I never forgot that moment."

Archambo now lives near Black Lake, where spearing sturgeon is just as much a tradition as it is on Lake Winnebago, although the lower numbers of fish necessitate a much smaller harvest—only five sturgeon can be taken from the lake each year.

Around ten years ago, Archambo read that the state of Michigan was considering closing down all harvest of sturgeon. She knew that would not be acceptable to a community where spearing had been going on for generations, so she transformed herself into the Michigan version of Bill Casper, the founder of Sturgeon For Tomorrow. And she has been every bit as persistent as he was thirty years ago.

Just as it was in the Winnebago system, poaching was hurting the Black Lake sturgeon population. Archambo decided to start a Michigan chapter of Sturgeon For Tomorrow. She traveled to Wisconsin several times to meet with Bill Casper and the biologists and wardens at the Wisconsin DNR to learn the ins and outs of the program. Today, Archambo and the members of the Black Lake Chapter of Sturgeon For Tomorrow help conduct scientific research, coordinate a volunteer Sturgeon Guard program, serve on a sturgeon advisory council that they created, and organize fund-raising initiatives to support sturgeon research, conservation, and educational programming.

Archambo sees one of the group's most important duties as creating future sturgeon enthusiasts. "We bring children to the river to see the fish and let them be a part of it and take ownership in it, because our vision is out a good 100 to 150 years—and that's to have a world-class fishery like Lake Winnebago," she said.

Brenda Archambo founded the Black Lake, Michigan, chapter of Sturgeon For Tomorrow in 1998 after learning about the success of the organization in Wisconsin.

While Wisconsin is enjoying the fruits of more than one hundred years of sturgeon management and thirty years of citizen involvement, other states around the Great Lakes are at the beginning of a multigenerational effort to make the lake sturgeon king of the fishes once more. Both Manny and Archambo know they will never see the full results of their work, but they are committed to this goal nonetheless. And that is because somewhere along the way, they both developed a relationship with this leathery, whiskered fish.

There is a rich cultural history encircling the sturgeon of Lake Winnebago, and it continues to expand outward as more and more people see and learn for themselves just what makes this fish so special. One can only hope that as numbers of sturgeon increase throughout the Great Lakes, more people will understand how important it is to protect them, and the circle will expand even further, until it encompasses the entire region, perhaps everywhere in the world where sturgeon are found.

This is a fish that predates many of the lakes and rivers it swims in, lives as long we do, and whose future is entirely in our hands. When people all around the Great Lakes are able to develop a relationship with sturgeon, it's then that they will all become people of the sturgeon—just like the Winnebago spearers and the Menominee Indians; the state managers, biologists, and wardens; the university researchers and educators; and the citizen volunteers who guard the riverbank or simply kneel at the water's edge with their children to gaze at an ancient fish.

Appendix

Much of the history and details of sturgeon spearing in the Lake Winnebago region chronicled in this book was gathered through oral history interviews conducted by volunteers throughout the community. This work is part of the Winnebago Sturgeon History Project, coordinated by the Wisconsin Department of Natural Resources with assistance from Sturgeon For Tomorrow and the University of Wisconsin Center for the Study of Upper Midwestern Cultures. These interviews, along with donated artifacts and photographs, will be archived at the Oshkosh Public Museum in Oshkosh, Wisconsin.

John Abler
Lynn and Larry Benedict
Gene Biettler
Gwen Bowe
Richard Braasch
Bill Buksyk
Ben Burg
Don Burg
Eric Cheslock
Russell Collar
Barb and Dennis Cook
Ken Corbett
Haze Diemel Jr.
Ron Epprecht
Dan Folz
Bob Frank
Dan Gerhardt
Vern and Karla Gebhart
Bill Goeser
Ed Gorchals
Dan Groeschel
Irene Halfmann
Rose and Norb Hartman
Eugene Herubin
Reuben Hoelzel
Wayne Hoelzel

Darlene and Bob Homan
Clarence Hopp
Willard Jenkins
John Jurgenson
Carl Jersild
Harry Kachur
Dick Koerner
Elmer Kuchenbecker
David Kuhn
Dorothy and Art Levknecht
Bill McAloon
James Nadler
Jerry Neumueller
Donald Peterson
Gordon Priegel
Mike Primising
LeRoy Remme
Mike Remme
George Schmidt
Vic and Mary Lou Schneider
Clarence Schroven
Pete Schuh
Al Schumacher
Art Sonnenberg
Henry Theisen
Ron Vanderzanden

Clem Van Gompel
Gerald Van Straten
Estelle Wagner
Cynthia Wendt
Linda Wendt
Mike Wendt
Shawn Wendt
Mike Will
Bob Wilson
Tom Wirth
Daniel Wollersheim
Howard Wruck
Ann Marie Ziemer

VOLUNTEER INTERVIEWERS

Ross Bielema
Patricia Braasch
Richard Braasch
Bill Casper
Eugene Herubin
Dick Koerner
Bill McAloon
Paul Muche
Dick Ristow
Howard Wruck

Timeline of Lake Winnebago
Sturgeon Management History

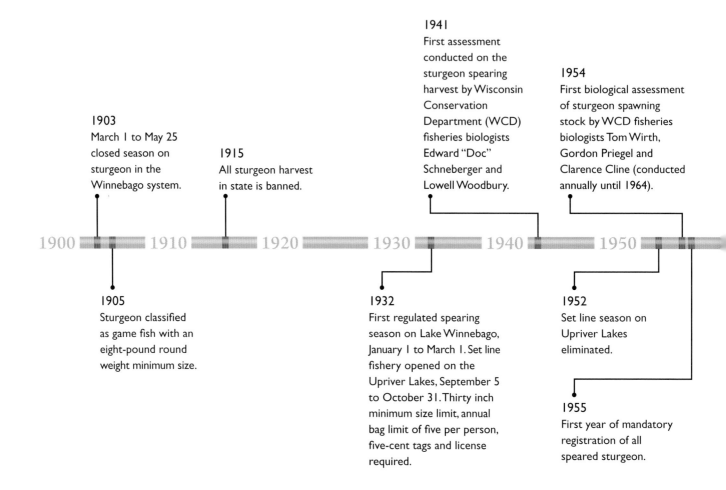

1941
First assessment conducted on the sturgeon spearing harvest by Wisconsin Conservation Department (WCD) fisheries biologists Edward "Doc" Schneberger and Lowell Woodbury.

1954
First biological assessment of sturgeon spawning stock by WCD fisheries biologists Tom Wirth, Gordon Priegel and Clarence Cline (conducted annually until 1964).

1903
March 1 to May 25 closed season on sturgeon in the Winnebago system.

1915
All sturgeon harvest in state is banned.

1900 1910 1920 1930 1940 1950

1905
Sturgeon classified as game fish with an eight-pound round weight minimum size.

1932
First regulated spearing season on Lake Winnebago, January 1 to March 1. Set line fishery opened on the Upriver Lakes, September 5 to October 31. Thirty inch minimum size limit, annual bag limit of five per person, five-cent tags and license required.

1952
Set line season on Upriver Lakes eliminated.

1955
First year of mandatory registration of all speared sturgeon.

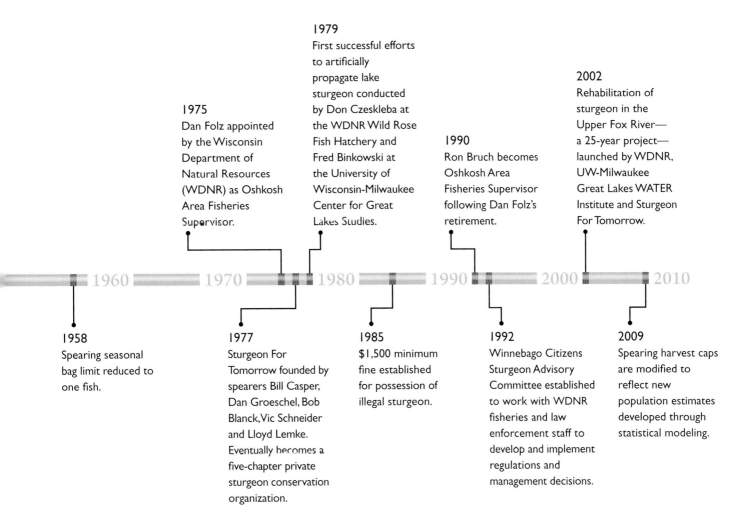

1979
First successful efforts to artificially propagate lake sturgeon conducted by Don Czeskleba at the WDNR Wild Rose Fish Hatchery and Fred Binkowski at the University of Wisconsin-Milwaukee Center for Great Lakes Studies.

1975
Dan Folz appointed by the Wisconsin Department of Natural Resources (WDNR) as Oshkosh Area Fisheries Supervisor.

1990
Ron Bruch becomes Oshkosh Area Fisheries Supervisor following Dan Folz's retirement.

2002
Rehabilitation of sturgeon in the Upper Fox River—a 25-year project—launched by WDNR, UW-Milwaukee Great Lakes WATER Institute and Sturgeon For Tomorrow.

1960   1970   1980   1990   2000   2010

1958
Spearing seasonal bag limit reduced to one fish.

1977
Sturgeon For Tomorrow founded by spearers Bill Casper, Dan Groeschel, Bob Blanck, Vic Schneider and Lloyd Lemke. Eventually becomes a five-chapter private sturgeon conservation organization.

1985
$1,500 minimum fine established for possession of illegal sturgeon.

1992
Winnebago Citizens Sturgeon Advisory Committee established to work with WDNR fisheries and law enforcement staff to develop and implement regulations and management decisions.

2009
Spearing harvest caps are modified to reflect new population estimates developed through statistical modeling.

Notes

Chapter 1

1. Lake sturgeon are also native to the Hudson Bay watershed.

2. N. A. Auer, "Importance of Habitat and Migration to Sturgeons with Emphasis on Lake Sturgeon," *Can. J. Fish. Aquat. Sci.* 53 (1996 Suppl. 1): 152–160; B. Gunderman and R. Elliott, "Assessment of Remnant Lake Sturgeon Populations in the Green Bay Basin, 2002–2003," *Report to the Great Lakes Fishery Trust* (2004), Project Number 2001.113.

3. E. M. Hay-Chmielewski and G. E. Whelan, eds., "Lake Sturgeon Rehabilitation Strategy," *Management Report of the Lake Sturgeon Committee* (1997), Fisheries Division, Michigan Department of Natural Resources, Ann Arbor, Michigan (quoted from Gunderman and Elliott, "Assessment of Remnant Lake Sturgeon Populations," 1).

4. WJK Harkness and J. R. Dymond, *The Lake Sturgeon: The History of Its Fishery and Problems of Conservation* (Ontario: Ontario Department of Lands and Forests, 1961).

5. Margaret Beattie Bogue, *Fishing the Great Lakes* (Madison: University of Wisconsin Press, 2000), 157.

6. *U.S. Commission of Fish and Fisheries Report*, 1887, 249.

7. National Park Service, *Southern New Jersey and the Delaware Bay: Historic Themes and Resources within the New Jersey Coastal Heritage Trail Route*, www.nps.gov/history/history/online_books/nj2/chap3b.htm; Richard Adams Carey, *The Philosopher Fish: Sturgeon, Caviar and the Geography of Desire* (New York: Counterpoint, 2006), 14.

8. Bogue, *Fishing the Great Lakes*, 159–160 (Bogue cites Milner, *U.S. Commission of Fish and Fisheries Report*, 1872); Wisconsin did take Milner's advice. On page 86 in the *Report of the Commissioner* for 1887, Oconto County is listed as producing 1,920 pounds of caviar and 150 pounds of isinglass in 1885.

9. Bogue, *Fishing the Great Lakes*, 160.

10. *U.S. Commission of Fish and Fisheries Report*, 1914, 66–67.

Chapter 2

1. Before the locks and dams were constructed, a determined adult lake sturgeon would have been capable of overcoming the four-foot height at the tallest drop near Kaukauna (personal observations by Ron Bruch and others on the Menominee Reservation). These intermittent defections could have helped boost the genetic diversity of the Winnebago population. However, after the river was dammed, the genetic exchange was limited to a one-way affair—while Lake Michigan sturgeon can no longer travel upstream to Lake Winnebago, tagged Winnebago sturgeon are still found in Green Bay as well as in Lakes Michigan, Huron, and Erie.

2. Randall Rohe, "Lumbering: Wisconsin's Northern Urban Frontier," in *Wisconsin Land and Life*, ed. Robert C. Ostergren and Thomas Vale, 225–231 (Madison: University of Wisconsin Press, 1997).

3. The fish in the Lake Winnebago System are among the cleanest in the state. Much of the industry that developed in towns and cities along the Winnebago System waterway were associated with the logging industry, such as sawmills and furniture stores. Very few heavy industrial plants were built on the waters; therefore, conventional pollutants such as PCBs (polychlorinated biphenyls) were not dumped into the Lake Winnebago as they were downstream in the Lower Fox River. The Fox Valley and its large concentration of paper mills and other heavy industry from Menasha down to Green Bay are all downstream of Lake Winnebago and the water quality problems experienced there historically did not impact Lake Winnebago or the waters upstream of the lake. Also, because Lake Winnebago and the Upriver Lakes sit on a limestone bedrock base, the water is slightly alkaline, which makes it difficult for mercury fallout from the atmosphere and natural background mercury to move into the food chain. All of this results in relatively low levels of the contaminants in Winnebago fish, including the lake sturgeon, a fish that in polluted waters, because of its fattiness and longevity, would be a sink for chemical contaminants.

4. Interview with B. O. Webster, 1961. Wisconsin State Historical Society SC968.

5. *Fifth Annual Report of the Commissioners of Fisheries of the State of Wisconsin for the Year Ending December 31, 1878*, 5, 7, 23.

6. Ibid., 5.

7. *Third Annual Report of the Commissioners of Fisheries of the State of Wisconsin for the Year 1876*, 10.

8. *Fish and Game Laws, Wisconsin, 1887*, compiled by Ernst G. Timme, secretary of state.

9. *Fish and Game Laws of the State of Wisconsin, 1892*, compiled and published under the direction of T. J. Cunningham, secretary of state.

10. *Fish and Game Laws of Wisconsin, 1899*, compiled under the direction of James T. Ellarson, state fish and game warden.

11. Barney Devine, chief conservation warden, to Dr. W.C. Wise, past president of the Fond du Lac chapter of Izaak Walton League, letter, January 15, 1935, Series 271, Box 753, Folder 1, Wisconsin Historical Society Archives.

12. www.wisconsinhistory.org/turningpoints/tp-033/?action=more_essay.

13. Robert Gough, *Farming the Cutover: A Social History of Northern Wisconsin, 1900–1949* (Lawrence: University Press of Kansas, 1997), 14.

14. *Wisconsin Wildlife Primer*, www.dnr.state.wi.us/org/land/wildlife/publ/wildlifeprimam.pdf.

15. William Mauthe, "Lake Winnebago" (speech given while chair of the Wisconsin Conservation Commission, undated), Wis Mss AA, Box 1, Wisconsin Historical Society Archives.

16. "Municipal Court Takes Up 5 Cases at Monday Session," *Appleton Post-Crescent*, April 30, 1923, 16.

17. "Sturgeon Case in Court: Trial of Winneconne Man Is in Progress Today—The Testimony of the Defendant," *Oshkosh Daily Northwestern*, June 25, 1915, 2.

18. "Shipped Fish in Trunks," *Oshkosh Daily Northwestern*, March 29, 1916, 6.

19. "Sportsmen Favor Sturgeon Fishing," *Appleton Post Crescent*, February 22, 1930, 12.

20. Gov. Philip F. La Follette to the senate, letter, April 1, 1931, Secretary of State Elections and Records, Legislative Bills—Senate Bills 1836–1931, Series No. 159, Box 305, Wisconsin Historical Archives.

21. Paul D. Kelleter to Gov. Philip F. La Follette, letter, March 30, 1931, Philip Fox La Follette Papers 1876–1973, Wis Mss Qs, Box 7, Wisconsin Historical Society Archives.

22. Ibid., March 31, 1931.

23. Committee on Conservation meeting, April 30, 1931, 2:00 p.m., Assembly Parlors. Series 159, Box 312, Bill 322S 1931, Wisconsin Historical Society Archives.

24. Donald Young, ed., *Adventures in Politics: The Memoirs of Philip LaFollette*, (Chicago: Holt, Rhinehart and Winston, 1970), 147.

25. B. O. Webster, "Proposed Fishing Regulations—Inland Waters," July 14, 1934, Series 271, Box 738, Folder 7, Wisconsin Historical Society Archives.

26. Excerpts of transcript of state meeting of conservation committees held at Madison, Wisconsin, on July 12 and 13, 1938, Series 271, Box 753, Folder 2, Wisconsin Historical Society Archives.

27. Resolution, December 28, 1938, Series 271, Box 753, Folder 3, Wisconsin Historical Society Archives.

28. H. W. MacKenzie to Julius P. Heil, letter, January 11, 1939, Series 271, Box 753, Folder 3, Wisconsin Historical Society Archives.

29. Public hearing relative to modification of Conservation Commission Order No. F-335 dealing with ice fishing regulations, January 17, 1939, Series 271, Box 753, Folder 3, Wisconsin Historical Society Archives.

30. Ibid.

31. Reply to resolution of Calumet County Sportsmen's Club from the Wisconsin Conservation Department, January 10, 1939, Series 271, Box 753, Folder 3, Wisconsin Historical Society Archives.

Chapter 3

1. William Radcliffe, *Fishing from the Earliest Times*, 1974. (Chicago: Ares Publishers Inc.).

2. David R.M. Beck, "Return to Namä'o Uskíwämît: The Importance of Sturgeon in Menominee History," *Wisconsin Magazine of History* 79, no. 1 (Autumn 1995): 41.

3. Beck, "Return to Namä'o Uskíwämît: The Importance of Sturgeon in Menominee History," 43.

4. Samuel Mazzuchelli. *The Memoirs of Father Samuel Mazzuchelli, O.P.* (Chicago: Priory Press, 1967).

5. "Fish for a Living," *Oshkosh Daily Northwestern*, January 11, 1895, 1.

6. J. O. Roorbach, "Fish-Spearing Through the Ice," in *The Boy's Book of Sports and Outdoor Life*, ed. Maurice Thompson, 322 (New York: The Century Co., 1886).

7. Ibid., 322–323.

8. Brenner Perryman, "The Economic Dimensions of the Lake Winnebago Lake Sturgeon Spear Fishery" (master's thesis, UW–Green Bay, 2004).

Chapter 4

1. Ben Apfelbaum, Eli Gottlieb, and Steven J. Michaan, *Beneath the Ice: The Art of the Spearfishing Decoy* (New York: E. P. Dutton in association with the Museum of American Folk Art, 1990), 8.

2. Ron Deiss, *Ice Spear Fishing: Focusing on the Upper Mississippi River La Crosse Reach* (Rock Island, IL: United States Army Corps of Engineers, 2005).

3. www.fishdecoy.com/spears.html.

Chapter 5

1. Wisconsin Department of Natural Resources, *Lake Sturgeon Harvest, Growth and Recruitment in Lake Winnebago, Wisconsin*, Technical Bulletin No. 83, Madison, WI, 1975, 19.

2. William P. Casper to James Addis, letter, March 22, 1977, Department of Natural Resources, Bill Casper Papers, private collection.

3. Douglas Martin, "W. W. Ballard, 92, Scholar with Wide Interests," *New York Times*, September 24, 1998.

4. Barney Crozier, "Vermont Senator's Speech Heralded McCarthy's End," *Barre Montpelier Times Argus*, August 29, 1979.

5. W. E. Lange, "Sturgeon Propagation Attempt," New London, WI, April 28, 1978; Bill Casper Papers, private collection.

6. Bill Ballard to James T. Addis, letter, February 6, 1979; Bill Casper Papers, private collection.

7. Arlene Buttles, "Hatchery Manager Retires," *Central Wisconsin Resorter*, March 11, 1987, 30.

8. James T. Addis to John H. Klingbiel, letter, February 14, 1980, Series 2550, Box 125, Folder 125/3, Wisconsin Historical Society Archives.

9. James T. Addis to Bill Casper, letter, March 26, 1980; Bill Casper Papers, private collection.

Chapter 6

1. Patty Loew, *Indian Nations of Wisconsin: Histories of Endurance and Renewal* (Madison: Wisconsin Historical Society Press, 2001), 30.

2. Ronald L. Trosper, "Indigenous Influence on Forest Management on the Menominee Indian Reservation," *Forest Ecology and Management* 249 (2007): 136.

3. Loew, *Indian Nations of Wisconsin*, 39.

4. Felix M. Keesing, *Menomini Indians of Wisconsin*, (Philadelphia: American Philosophical Society, 1939), 141.

5. Ibid., 148.

6. Ibid.

7. John Lawe to James Porlier, letter, February 3, 1820, Collections of the State Historical Society of Wisconsin, vo. 20 (Madison, WI, 1911), 332.

8. *Travels and Explorations of the Jesuit Missionaries in New France, 1610–1791*, edited by Reuben Gold Thwaites, computerized transcription by Tomasz Mentrak (Cleveland, OH: The Burrows Brothers Company, 1899), 272–274.

9. www.wisconsinhistory.org/turningpoints/search.asp?id=901.

10. *The Indian Tribes of the Upper Mississippi Valley and Region of the Great Lakes*, edited and translated by Emma Helen Blair (Cleveland, OH: Arthur Clark, 1911), 304.

11. Quote from tribal member Weshonaquet Mosehart in deposition in Keshena, August 25, 1913, interpreter Reginald Oshkosh, witnesses Reginald Oshkosh and Frank Wilber, Menominee Historic Preservation Department. In Beck, "Return to Namä'o Uskíwämît," 45.

12. J. L. Whitehouse, "A History of the Wolf River and Its Pioneers," 1947 and 1948–1949, Book 8, p. 3, SC 2655, Wisconsin Historical Society, Madison, WI.

13. A. Smith, "A Big Sturgeon Hunt," *The Wisconsin State Register*, May 23, 1863, 1.

14. *Milwaukee Sentinel*, May 3, 1877, 2.

15. Alanson Skinner, "Material Culture of the Menomini," in F. W. Hodge, ed., *Indian Notes and Monographs*, vol. 20 (New York: Museum of the American Indian, Heye Foundation, 1921), 205–206.

16. Phebe Jewell Nichols, "Indians Contributed Much to World Agricultural Wealth," *Appleton Post-Crescent*, December 12, 1939, 19.

17. Kathy McDonough with assistance from David Grignon, "Menominee Indian Tribe of Wisconsin: The Importance to Menominee Culture and Tradition," in Beck, "Return to Namä'o Uskíwämît," 37.

18. Beck, "Return to Namä'o Uskíwämît," 40.

19. *Statutes of the Territory of Wisconsin, Passed by the Legislative Assembly Thereof, at a Session Commencing in November 1838, and at an Adjourned Session Commencing in January, 1839* (Albany, NY: Packard, Van Benthuysen and Co., 1839), 121.

20. Wisconsin Department of Natural Resources, *History of Dams in Wisconsin*, http://dnr.wi.gov/org/water/wm/dsfm/dams/history.html.

21. *Fourth Annual Report of the Commissioners of Fisheries of the State of Wisconsin, for the Fiscal Year Ending September 30, 1877*, 4–5.

22. *Laws of Wisconsin 1907*. Chapter 488, Section 14971; there was a previous two-year period when a fishway law existed. In 1895 a law was passed to require, by the following spring, "fishways in the dams on and across all streams in the state of Wisconsin." Unfortunately, as pointed out by the fish commissioners the next year, most dam owners didn't hear about the law until after the deadline to build the fishways had passed. There were problems with the law, too, they said. The legislature had set a cost limit of $150 to build a fishway, and this was unfeasible. It also laid the responsibility of regulation with the fish commissioners, who basically served as unpaid volunteers. They appealed to the legislature to modify the law; instead, it was repealed in 1897.

23. Beck, "Return to Namäo Uskíwämît," 46.

24. Annual Indian affairs round table, Oshkosh, WI, April 10, 1930, Series 271, Box 419, Folder 1, Wisconsin Historical Society, Madison, WI.

25. B. O. Webster to Ralph Friderlung, letter, April 11, 1935, Series No. 271, Box 668, Folder 4, Wisconsin Historical Society Archives, Madison, Wisconsin.

26. Russ Pyre, "Hook, Line and Sinker," *Wisconsin State Journal*, January 2, 1944, 23.

Chapter 7

1. Patty Murray, "Reviving an Ancient Fish," *The Environment Report*, October 8, 2001.

2. Richard Adams Carey, *The Philosopher Fish: Sturgeon, Caviar and the Geography of Desire* (New York: Counterpoint, 2006), 80.

3. E. A. Birge, "The Regulation of Fisheries," in *Third Biennial Report of the Conservation Commission of the State of Wisconsin*, 1912, 71.

4. William J. K. Harkness, "Report on Artificial Propagation of Sturgeon," University of Toronto., Series 271, Box 669, Folder 7, Wisconsin Historical Society Archives.

5. Edward Schneberger and Lowell A. Woodbury, "The Lake Sturgeon, *Asipenser Fulvescens Rafinesque*, in Lake Winnebago, Wisconsin," in *Transactions of the Wisconsin Academy of Sciences, Arts and Letters, Volume XXXVI* (Madison: Wisconsin Conservation Department, 1944), 132.

6. "Long-Range Study Will Aid Fishermen," *Oshkosh Daily Northwestern*, March 26, 1953, 30.

7. The Wisconsin Conservation Commission was first established by Chapter 644, Laws of 1911, as an uncompensated advisory body. The functions of the Board of Forestry, the Fish and Game Warden, the State Park Board, and the Commissioners of Fisheries were consolidated and vested in a new State Conservation Commission under Chapter 406, Laws of 1915. Initially, the full-time commissioners exercised responsibility for both policy making and the administration of conservation programs. In 1927, the commission became a part-time board devoted exclusively to setting conservation policy. Administration of conservation programs fell to the Conservation Department. When the Conservation Department was merged into the new Department of Natural Resources in 1967, the commission was abolished. Oversight of the new department became the responsibility of the Natural Resources Board.

8. Harkness, "Report on Artificial Propagation."

9. F. P. Binkowski and S. I. Doroshov, eds., *North American Sturgeons: Biology and Aquaculture Potential* (Boston: Dr W. Junk Publishers, 1985), 9.

Chapter 8

1. *Daily Free Democrat*, May 9, 1851, 3.

2. *Chicago Daily*, July 4, 1897, 24.

3. *Oshkosh Daily Northwestern*, June 21, 1906, 4.

Illustration Credits

All photographs © Bob Rashid unless otherwise credited. Photographs identified with WHi or WHS are from the Society's collections; address requests to reproduce these photos to the Visual Materials Archivist at the Wisconsin Historical Society, 816 State Street, Madison, WI 53706.

Front Matter

page iii sturgeon decoy **page vii** WDNR (Wisconsin Department of Natural Resources) staff and SFT (Sturgeon For Tomorrow) members **page viii** Jurgenson decoys; sturgeon spear; Corbett and Diemel **page ix** Mary Boettcher hugging sturgeon; George Schmidt decoy, from the Collections of the Oshkosh Public Museum, Oshkosh, Wisconsin. OPM Acc # 2007.15 (photo © Bob Rashid); Sturgeon Guard; license plate; Menominee powwow, Merissa Bloedorn; sturgeon netting; porpoising sturgeon; sturgeon eggs **page x** porpoising sturgeon

Chapter 1

pages 2 and 3 sturgeon map, courtesy of UW Sea Grant Institute **page 4** Ron Bruch at Wendt's **page 7** Ben and Don Burg; Stockbridge decoy **page 8** Winnebago watershed map, courtesy of UW Sea Grant Institute **page 9** sturgeon swimming, courtesy of Jennifer Hayes **page 11** juvenile lake sturgeon; adult lake sturgeon **page 12** sturgeon illustration, from *Cyclopaedia Icthyology* **page13** sturgeon illustration, courtesy of the New York State Department of Environmental Conservation; chariot-boat pulled by fish, from *The Faerie Queene* **page 15** flying fish, AP photo/Phil Sandlin **page 16** landing a sturgeon on the wharf, courtesy of University of Washington Libraries, Special Collections, Cobb 171 **page 18** sturgeon illustration, from *Cyclopaedia Icthyology* **page 19** Ojibwa canoe race, from *Illustrations of the Manners, Customs and Condition of the North American Indians* **page 21** WHi-19652, Newcomb Spoor **page 22** 1915 photo of sturgeon, courtesy of Mary Lou Schneider

Chapter 2

page 24 and 25 1867 map, section of Wisconsin and Fox River, courtesy of the American Geographical Society Library, University of Wisconsin–Milwaukee Libraries **page 26** WHi-61164, fish stocking railroad car **page 27** small sturgeon icon, courtesy of NOAA Historic Fisheries Collection **page 29** WHi-7287, men spearing sturgeon **page 30** WHi-38167, young boys on cutover land **page 32** Wardens Popple and Kraemer, courtesy of the WDNR (Wisconsin Department of Natural Resources) **page 34** WHi-61156, Warden Kramer and assistant removing illegal snag line from Wolf River **page 35** snag hook and treble hook, courtesy of Ron Bruch (photos ©Bob Rashid) **page 36** Robert Abraham **page 38** illegal catch: fisherman and sturgeon, courtesy of the New London Public Museum **page 41** 1947 wardens, courtesy of the WDNR **page 42** WHi-61160, "Battle of the Muskies" **page 45** Ken Corbett and Haze Diemel **page 48** metal sturgeon tags, from the collections of the Oshkosh Public Museum, Oshkosh, Wisconsin; OPM Acc#2007.15 **page 50** Dick Koerner **page 53** WHi-5748, Wisconsin billboard **page 54** WHi-61155, Warden Kramer and assistant with confiscated sturgeon and illegal snag lines **page 58** 1940 confiscation ticket, courtesy of Haze Diemel Jr. **page 60** original Goyke photograph, from the collections of the Oshkosh Public Museum, all rights reserved, Oshkosh, Wisconsin; OPM #P2002.081

Chapter 3

pages 62 and 63 truck on ice **page 64** WHi-2061, fisherman **pages 66 and 67** sturgeon in tank **page 68** wood decoy, from the collections of the Oshkosh Public Museum, Oshkosh, Wisconsin; OPM #NC -70 **page 69** WHi-(x3)40976, Indians spearing fish in water **page 70** mussel shell lure, from the collections of the Oshkosh Public Museum, Oshkosh, Wisconsin; OPM #1998.22.220; bone harpoon, from the collections of the Oshkosh Public Museum, Oshkosh, Wisconsin; OPM #2111-142; bone harpoon, from the collections of the Oshkosh Public Museum, Oshkosh, Wisconsin; OPM # 800-122

Chapter 4

Chapter 5

Chapter 6

Index

Page numbers in *italic* refer to illustrations.

population: commercial fishing and decline in, 21, 23, 26; early estimates, 56, 61; global decline of sturgeon, 209; harvest limits and sustainable, 220; "hole" left by over-exploitation of fisheries, 240; Lake Winnebago System as distinct biological, 26–27; research on sturgeon, 212, 215, 219; stocking to increase (*See* stocking fish)

"Porkchop" the sturgeon, 230

powwows, *198, 200, 202, 203, 204, 205*

Priegel, Gordon, 143, *220, 221*

Primising, Mike, 146, 223, *223*

Probst, Robert, 219

propagation, 182; diet for sturgeon larvae, 225; egg collection for, 134, 146–47, 148, *149, 227, 248, 250–51*; field fertilization for, *250–51*; milt collection for, *228,* 241; sturgeon eggs in lab, *227*

radio transmitters and tracking, *224, 225, 226, 228,* 230, *249*; PITs (passive integrated transponders), 216, *216, 226,* 257

Ragotzkie, Robert, 232

record-size fish, 81, 94, *95*

recreational fishing, 5; political advocacy groups and, 37; spearing as, 52, 74; tourism industry and, 49, 53

regulations: bag limits, 85, 104, 138, 222; citizens advisory groups and formation of, 154; compilation of state laws, 28; conditions prior to, 21, 23; conservation groups and, 31; exemptions to, 31, 49; fishways required by law, 282n22; gill netting prohibited by, 31; harvest limits, 220, 222, 238, 256; on ice shanties, 104; legislative process and development of, 50–51; licensing, 72, 104; Milldam Act and regulation of dams, 179–80; minimum size of catch (length), 104, 115, 138, 222, 238; need for uniform, 28, 49; opposition to, 28; as political issue, 31, 37, 43, 48, 50–51; popular opposition to, 49, 55–56; prohibited fishing methods, 33–34; registration of catch, 222, *252–59*; scientific management and, 5; season length, 104, 222; tagging requirements, 104; Wisconsin Conservation Commission and, 283n7.
See also enforcement of fishing regulations

Reinl, Ron, *157*

Reiter, Don, 182, *183*

Remme, Kay, 81

Remme, LeRoy, 74, 81, *81*

Remme, Mike, 81, 82

reproduction, 14, 17

research: aerial, *231*; data collection during catch registration, *252–59*; data collection during spawning, *135,* 241; embryology studies, 147–48; into life cycle of sturgeon, 147–48, 212, 226; for population research, 212, 215, 219; Sturgeon For Tomorrow and support for, 143–46, *145,* 150; on sturgeon propagation, 143–46, *145,* 148, 150, 225, 229; tags and tagging systems used in, 134, *192–93,* 216, *216–17,* 230; University of Wisconsin and, 148, *210,* 211–12, 232, *250*

Rinzel, Doug, *vii*

Ristow, Dick, *vii*

Ristow, Sandy, *vii*

Roorbach, J. O., 69, 72

Rosenthal, Harald, 234

Rost, Ben, *218*

St. Louis River, *268*

Schacht, John, 20

Schacht, Siemen, 20

Schaller, Todd, 156, *159*

Schlumpf, Charles, 212

Schmid, Jeanie, *84*

Schmidt, George, *114–15, 118*; on carving decoys, 118

Schneberger, Edward, 56, 61, *210,* 212, 213

Schneider, Mary Lou, 83, 85, 120, *141*; decoys carved by, *121*

Schneider, Tom, *113*

Schneider, Vic, 72, 80, 83, 143; caviar processing by, *98*

Schoebel, Leo A., 79

Schroeder, Elroy, *95*

Schroven, Jake, 122

Schwobe, Alexis, *84*

Schwobe, Wendy, *84*

scientific management, 5–6, *142,* 216; of fisheries by Menominee, 182; Fisheries Commission established, 28; harvest limits and sustainable populations, 220; hatchery propagation and,

KATHLEEN SCHMITT KLINE is a science writer at the University of Wisconsin Sea Grant Institute, which supports research, education, and outreach dedicated to the stewardship and sustainable use of the nation's Great Lakes and ocean resources. She has a B.A. in biology and English from Luther College in Decorah, Iowa, and an M.S. in life sciences communication from the University of Wisconsin–Madison.

RONALD M. BRUCH is Natural Resources Region Team Supervisor for the Wisconsin Department of Natural Resources, based in Oshkosh. He has been the lead sturgeon biologist for the Winnebago system since 1990. In his efforts to establish scientifically based sturgeon management policies with maximum public input, Bruch has worked with numerous local, state, tribal, federal, and international agencies and organizations. He has a Ph.D. in biology from the University of Wisconsin–Milwaukee.

FREDERICK P. BINKOWSKI is a senior scientist at the University of Wisconsin–Milwaukee Great Lakes WATER Institute and the aquaculture advisory services specialist with the University of Wisconsin Sea Grant Institute. He has been raising and researching lake sturgeon since 1979. Binkowski's research has focused on early life stage development, nutrition, and behavior—he is one of the first scientists to monitor sturgeon movements using radio and sonic telemetry. He has an M.S. in zoology from the University of Wisconsin–Milwaukee.

BOB RASHID (1949–2008) was a photographer/writer whose previous books include *Wisconsin's Rustic Roads*, *Backroads of Wisconsin*, and *Gone Fishing*. His first book, *Wisconsin's Rustic Roads*, inspired Wisconsin Public Television's documentary of the same title, and he worked as location photographer for three other television documentaries. An avid traveler, Rashid visited 19 countries and covered assignments in Europe, Asia and Central America. His work was published in *Time*, *Newsweek*, the *New York Times*, *Travel/Holiday* and Northwest Airlines *World Traveler*.